The Peak District

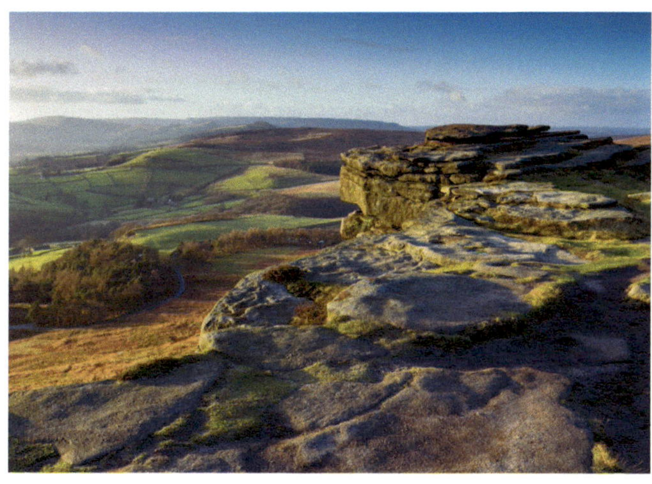

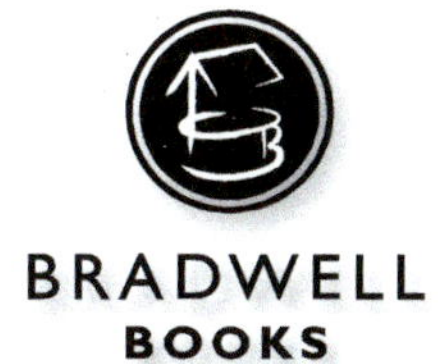

BRADWELL
BOOKS

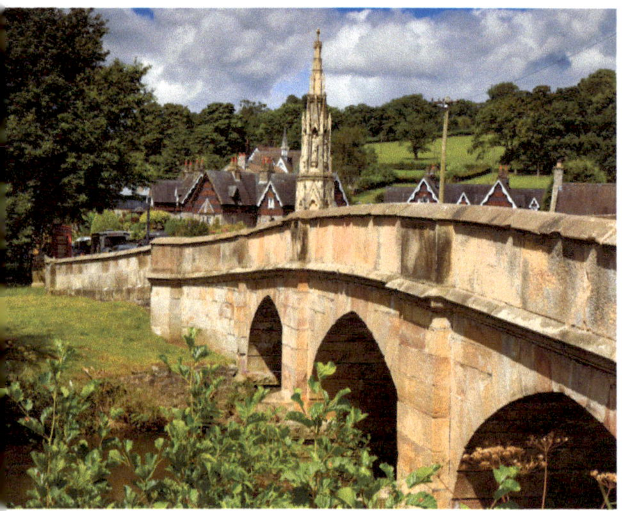

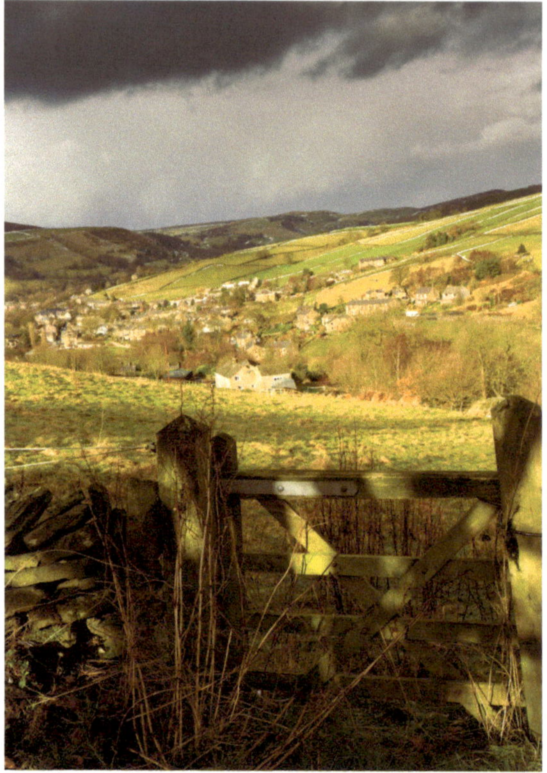

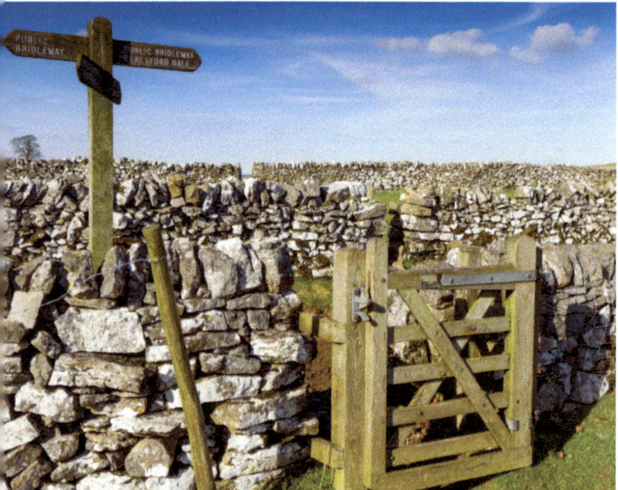

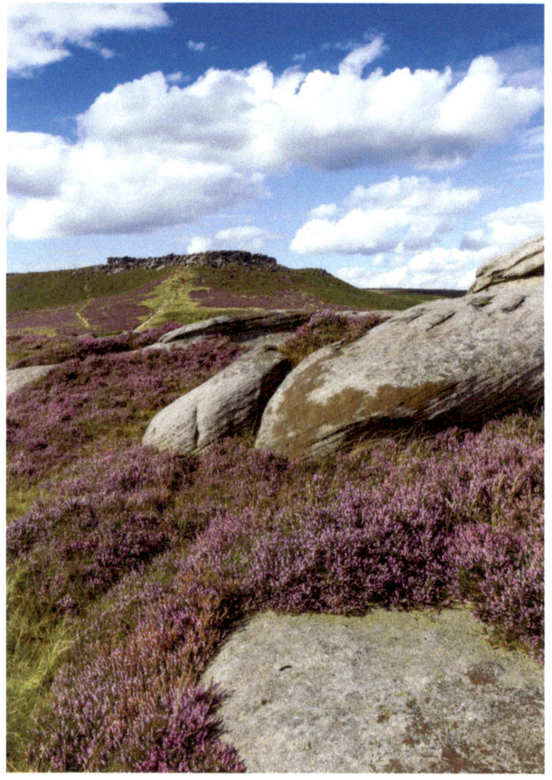

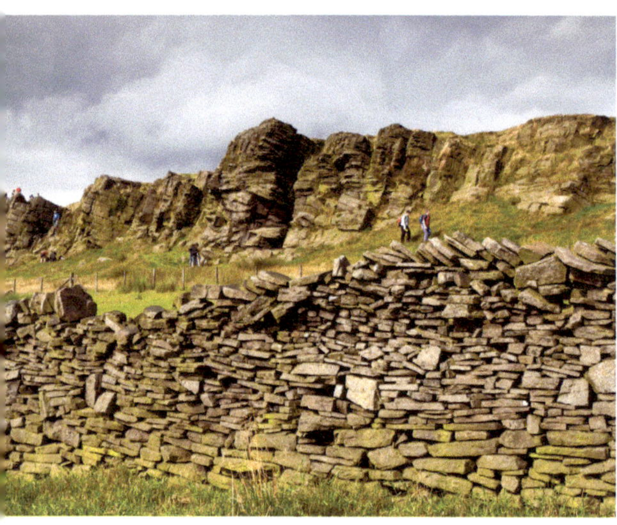

A TASTE OF THE PEAK DISTRICT

ILAM · HAYFIELD · HARTINGTON · GOYT VALLEY · HATHERSAGE

Welcome to **Bradwell's Images of The Peak District** – a lovingly prepared collection of photographs that cannot fail to whet your appetite to explore the region for yourself, and that we hope will act as a constant reminder of the sheer beauty of The Peak District.

Photographers, Susan & Andrew Caffrey, have a deep passion for the Peak District and its delightful landscape; a passion that is clearly reflected in each of these unique and stunning images. The book is divided into eight distinct areas, each with a short introductory paragraph outlining its main features; however, we think the photographs really speak for themselves. *Enjoy!*

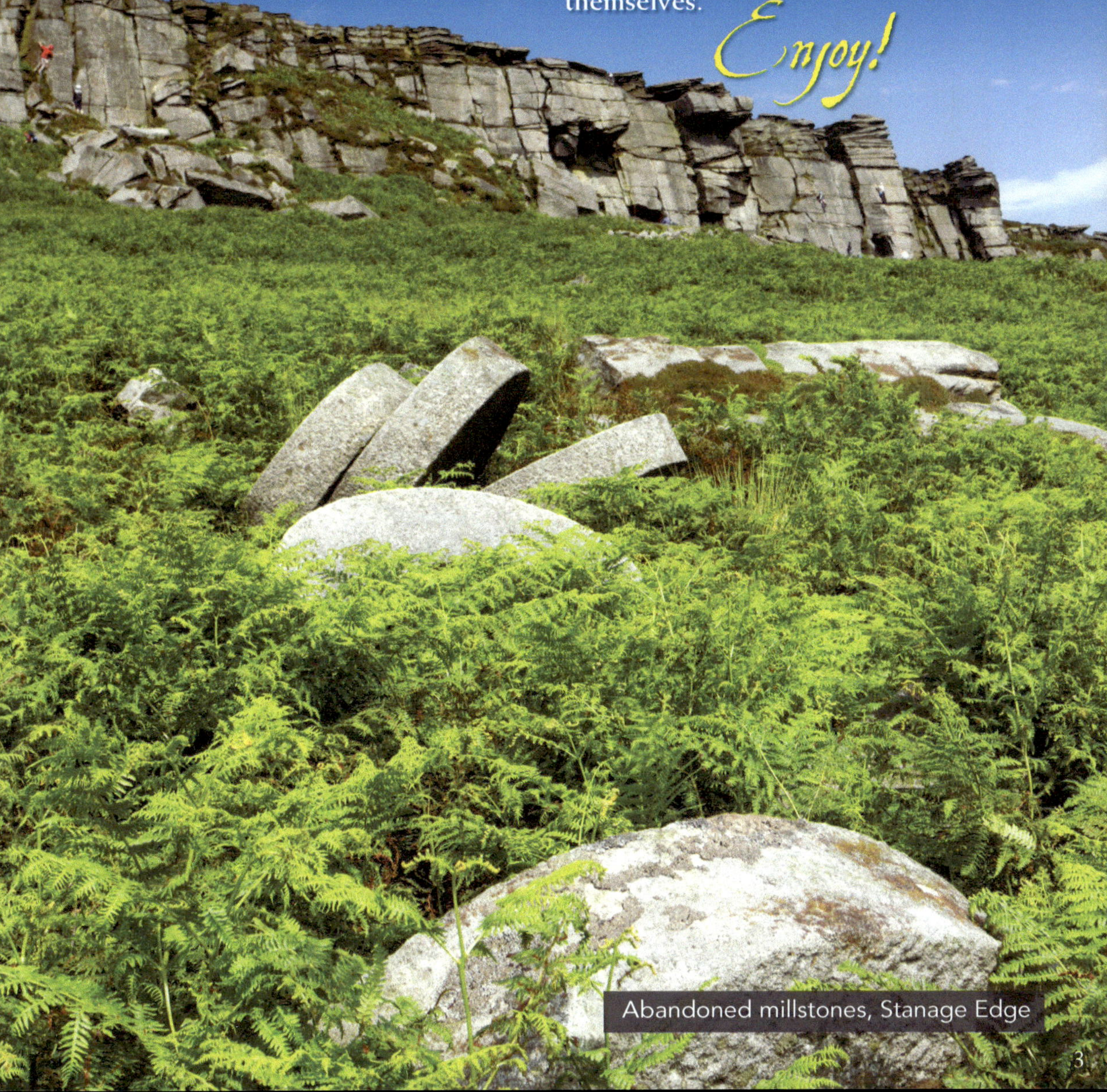

Abandoned millstones, Stanage Edge

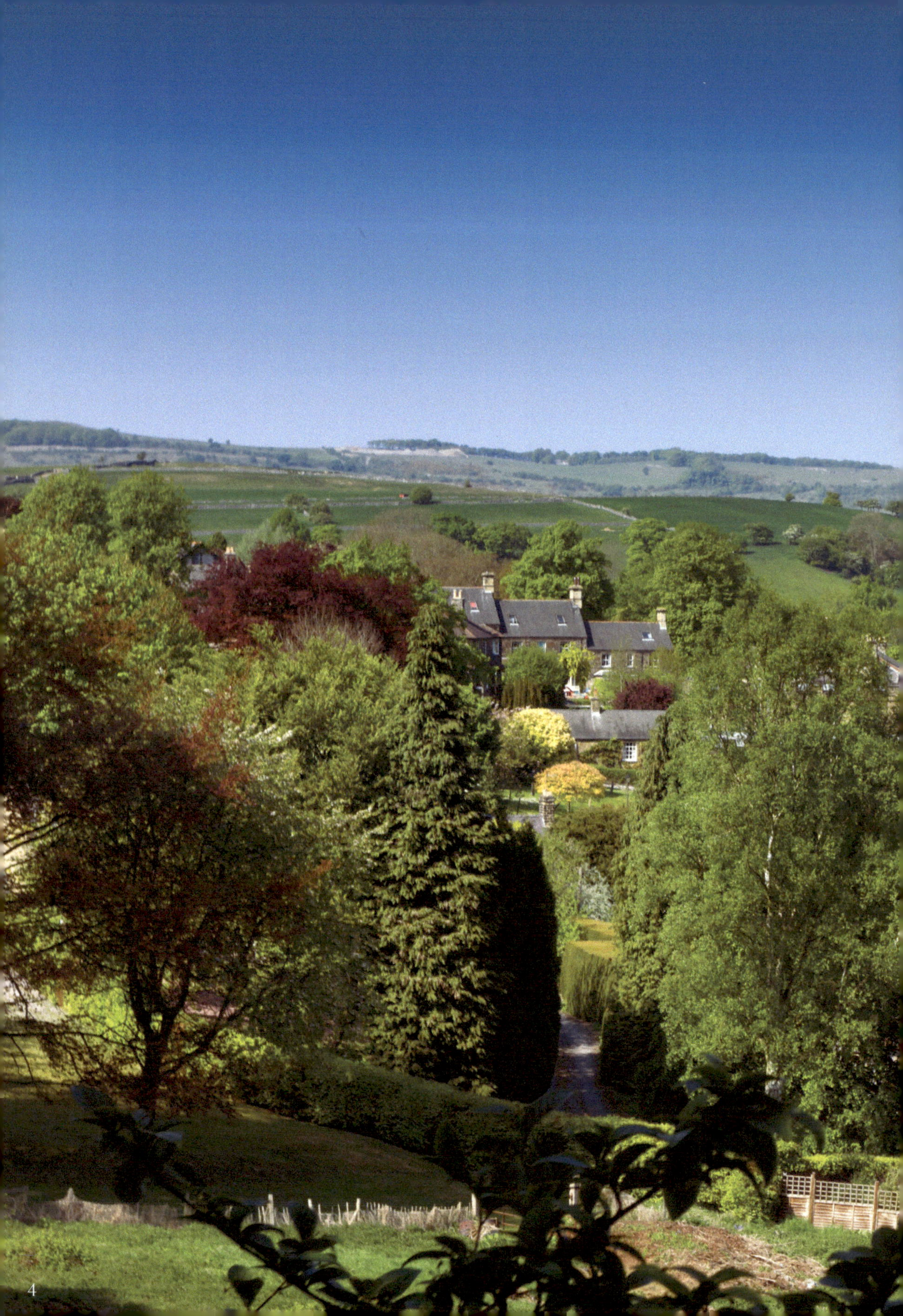

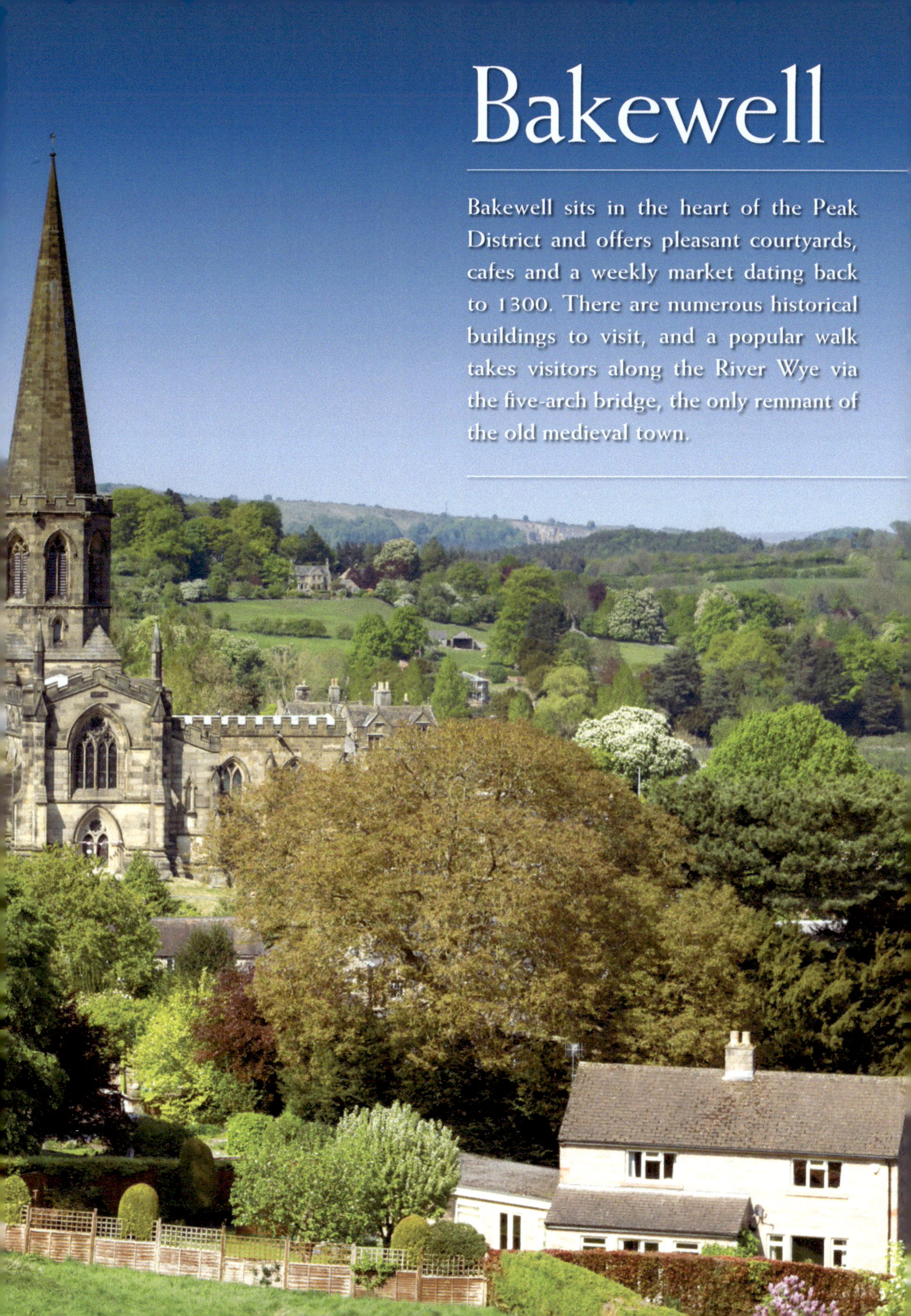

Bakewell

Bakewell sits in the heart of the Peak District and offers pleasant courtyards, cafes and a weekly market dating back to 1300. There are numerous historical buildings to visit, and a popular walk takes visitors along the River Wye via the five-arch bridge, the only remnant of the old medieval town.

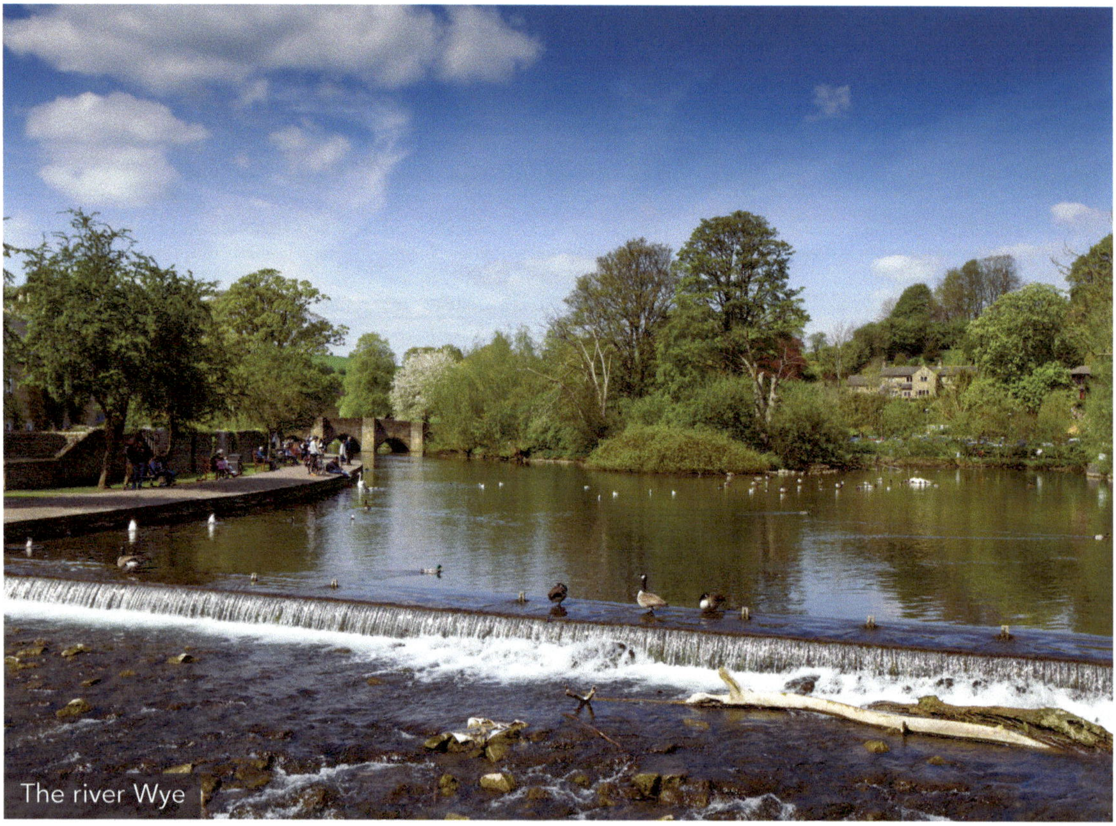

The river Wye

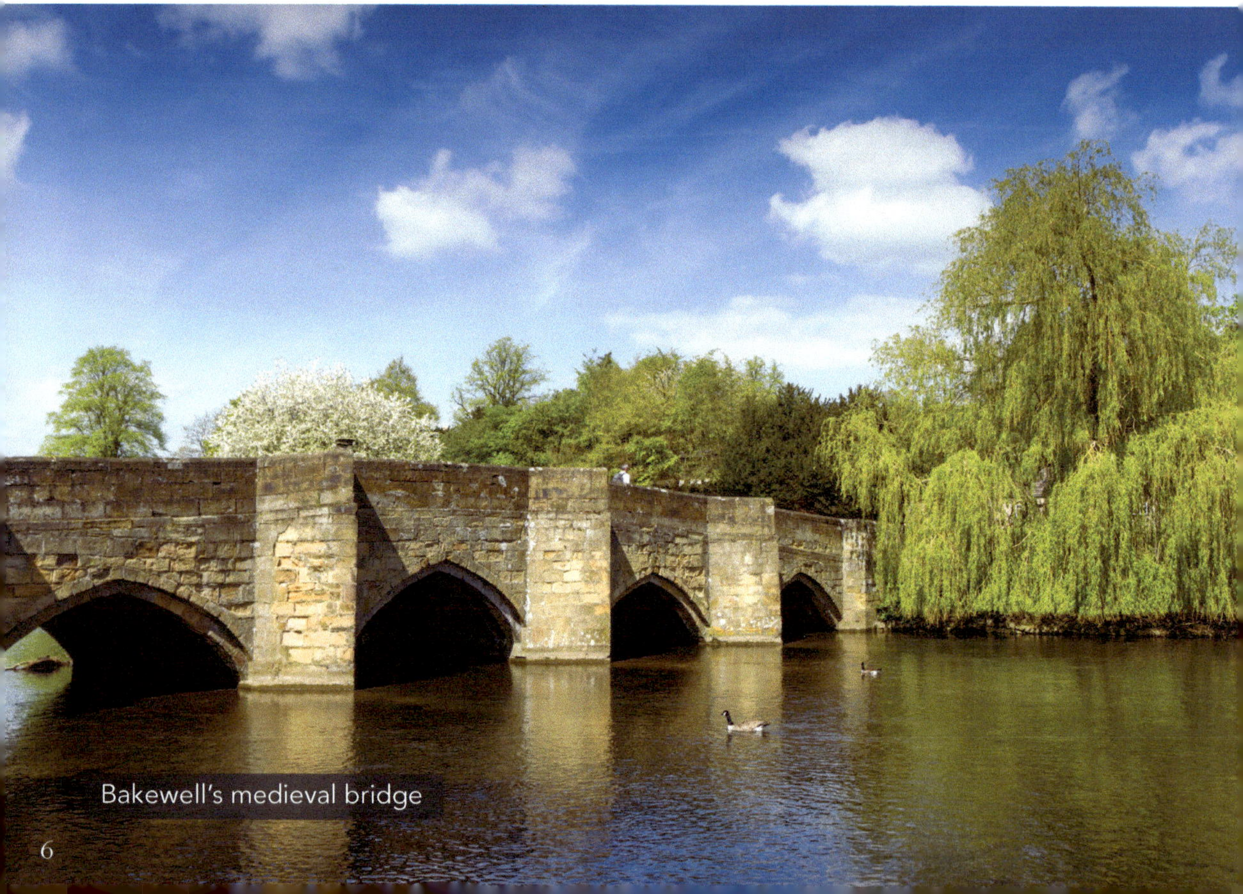

Bakewell's medieval bridge

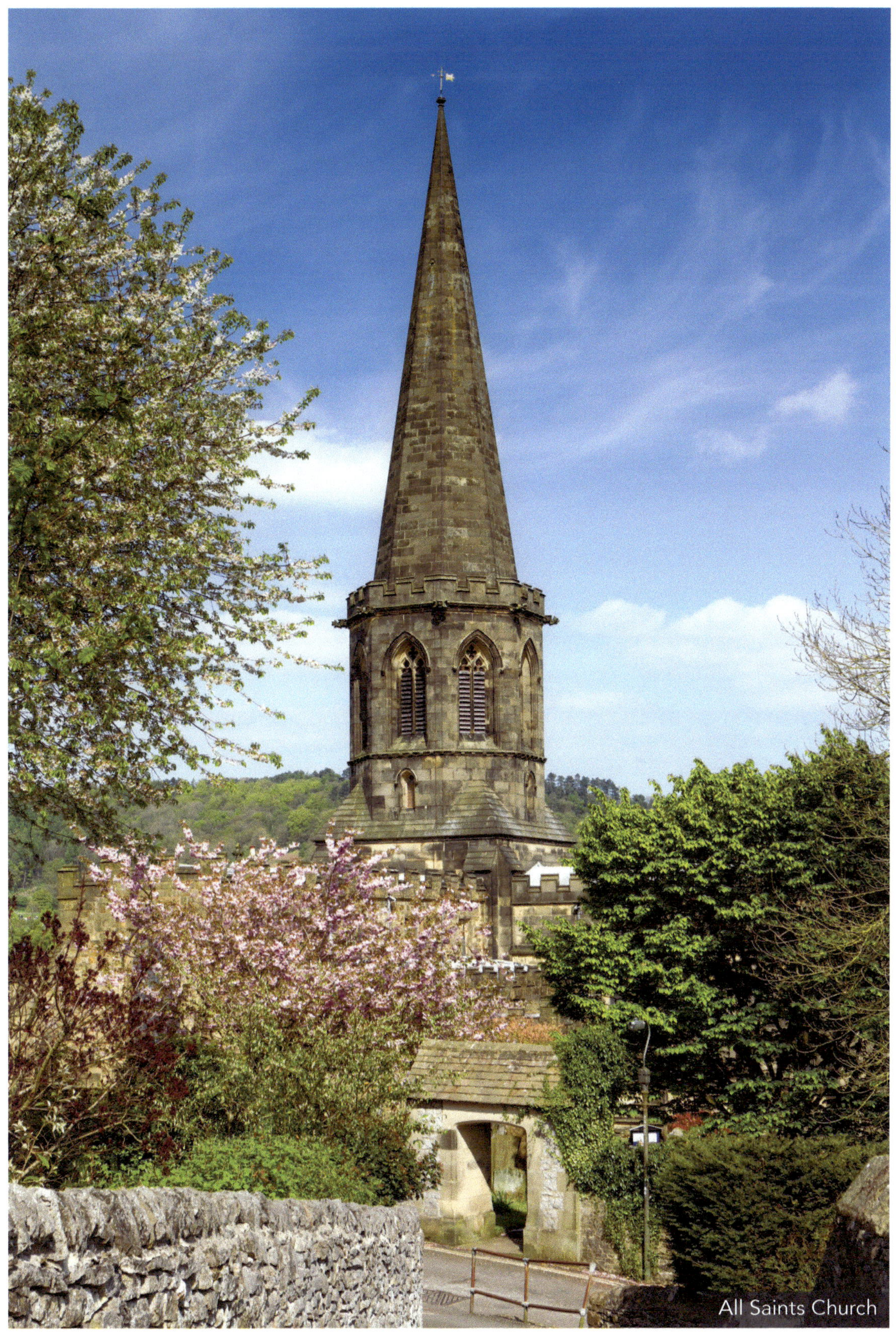
All Saints Church

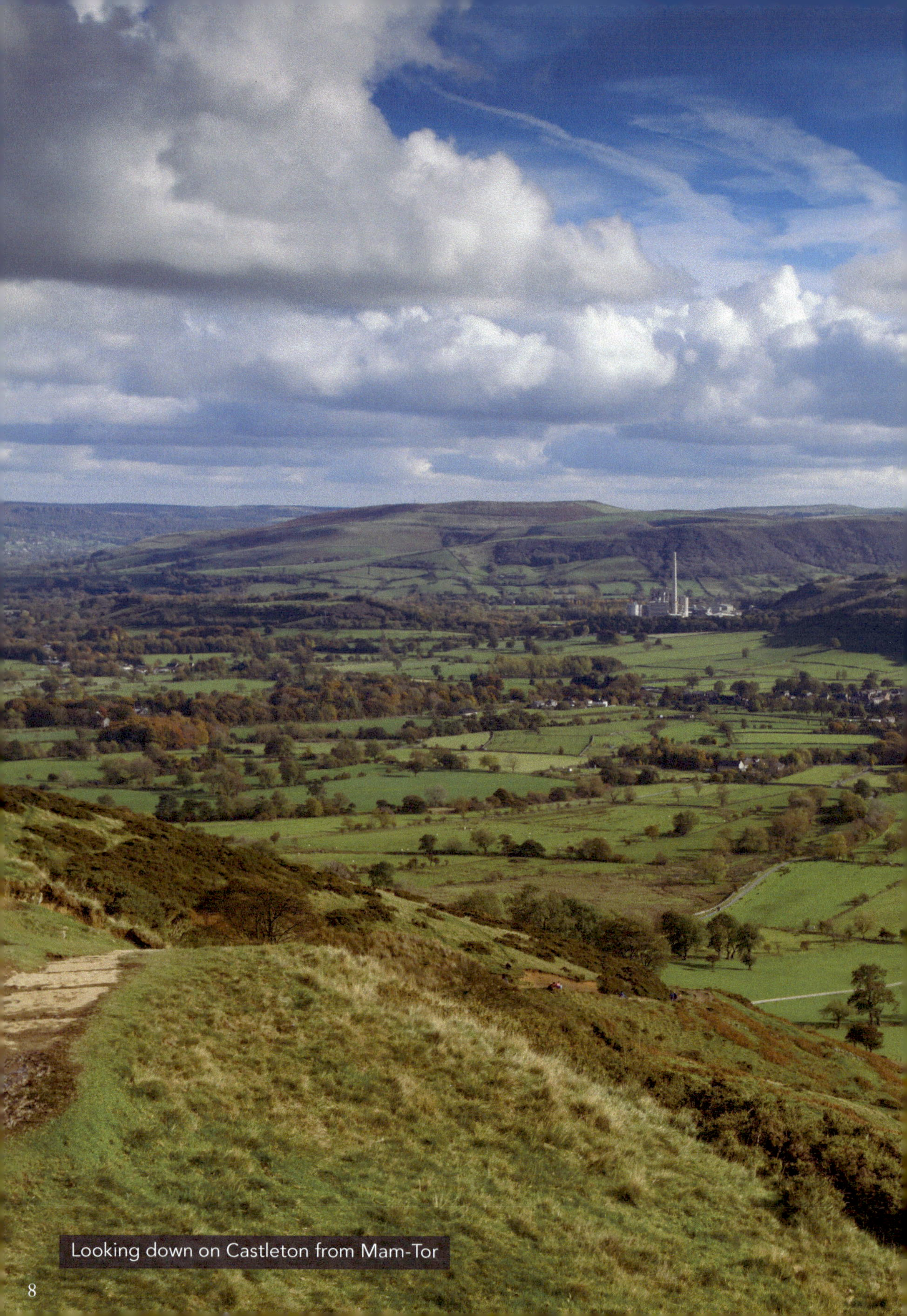

Looking down on Castleton from Mam-Tor

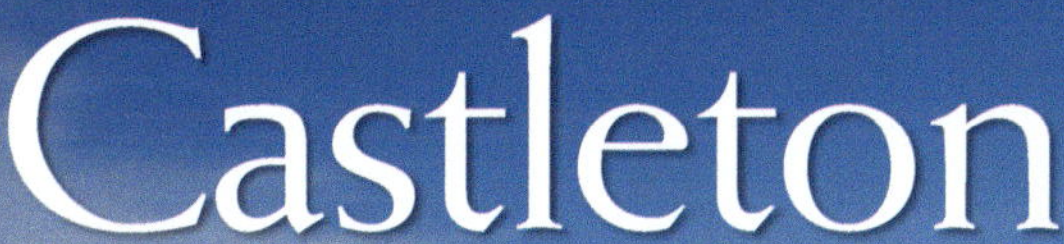

Castleton

The village of Castleton is surrounded by lush green countryside and overlooked by the impressive ruins of Peveril Castle. To the west, Mam Tor, the 'shivering mountain', is a favourite local walk, while magical caves of fossils and beautiful Blue John stone can be discovered by boat or on foot.

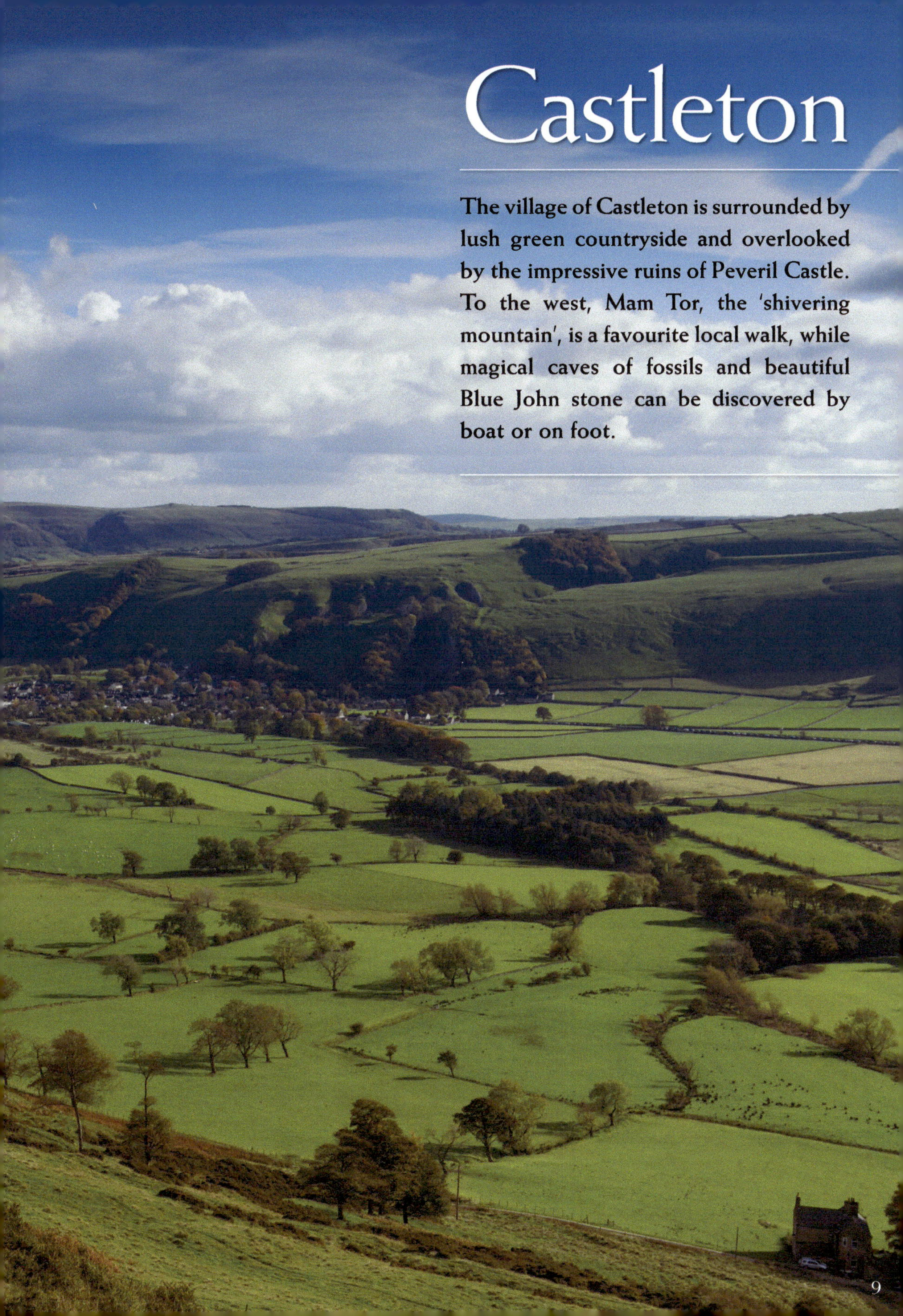

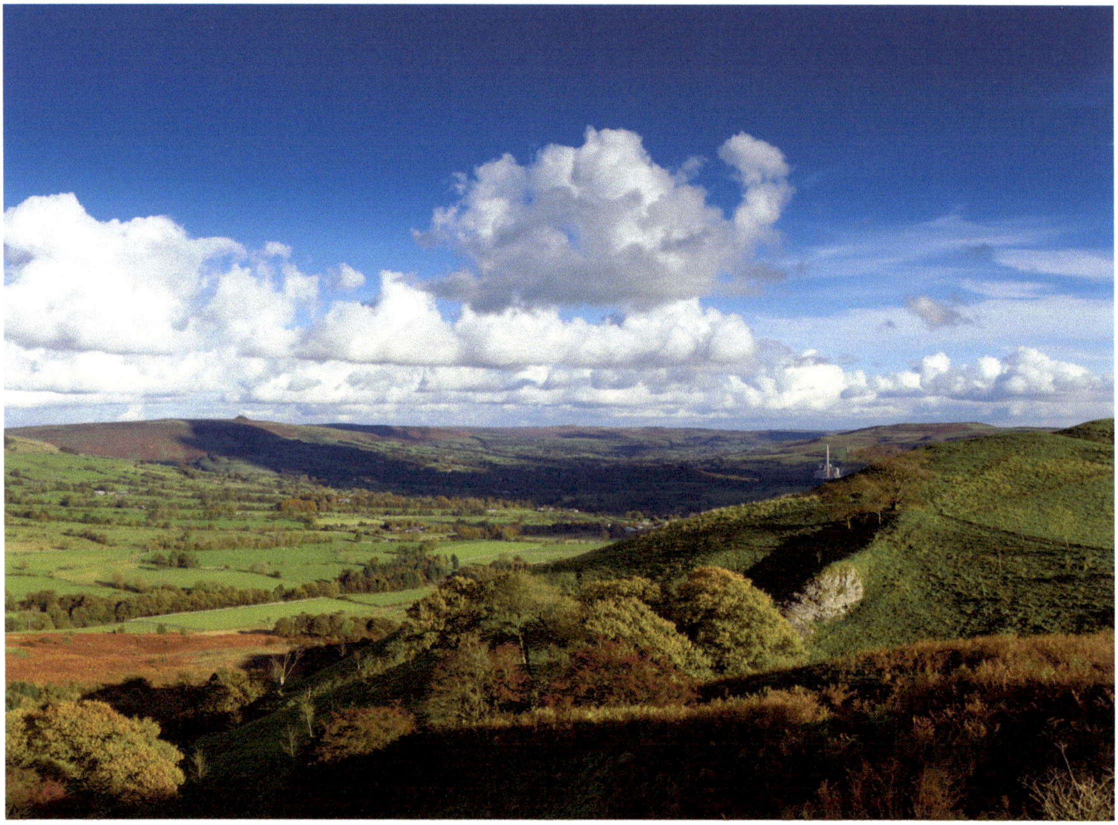

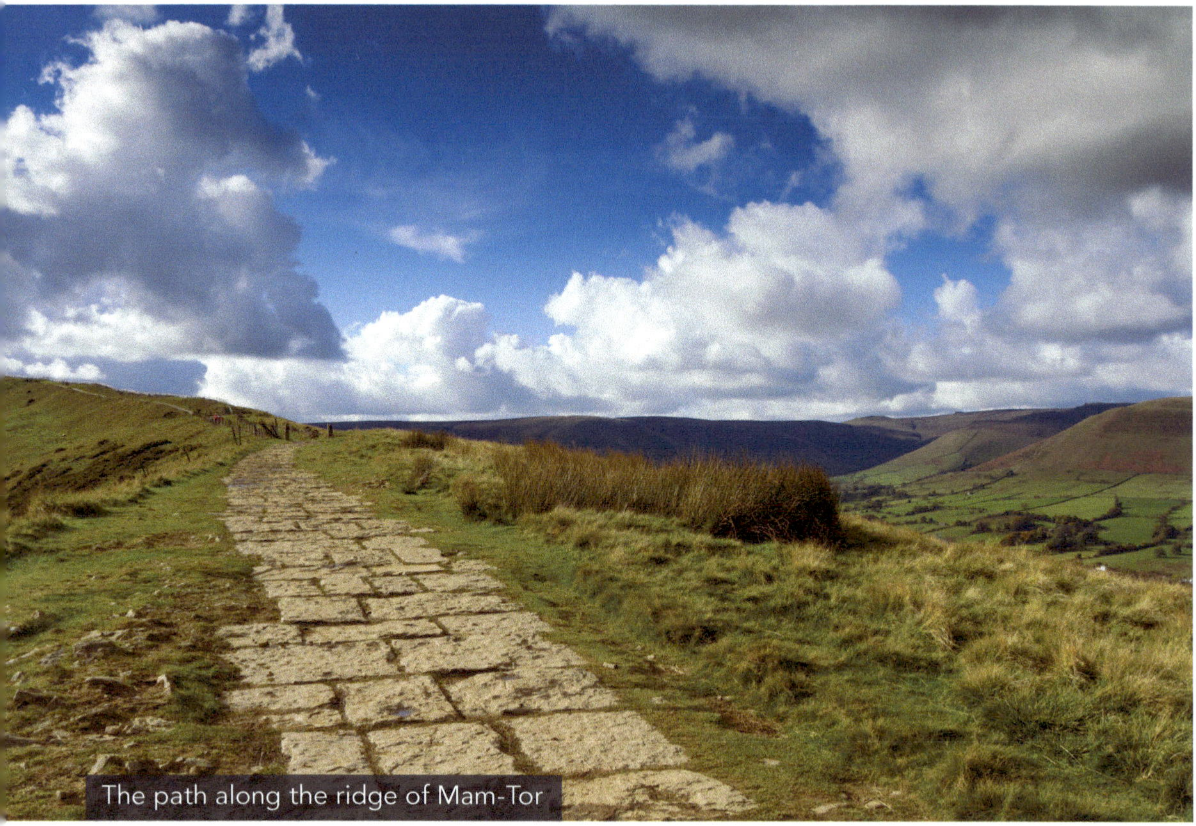

The path along the ridge of Mam-Tor

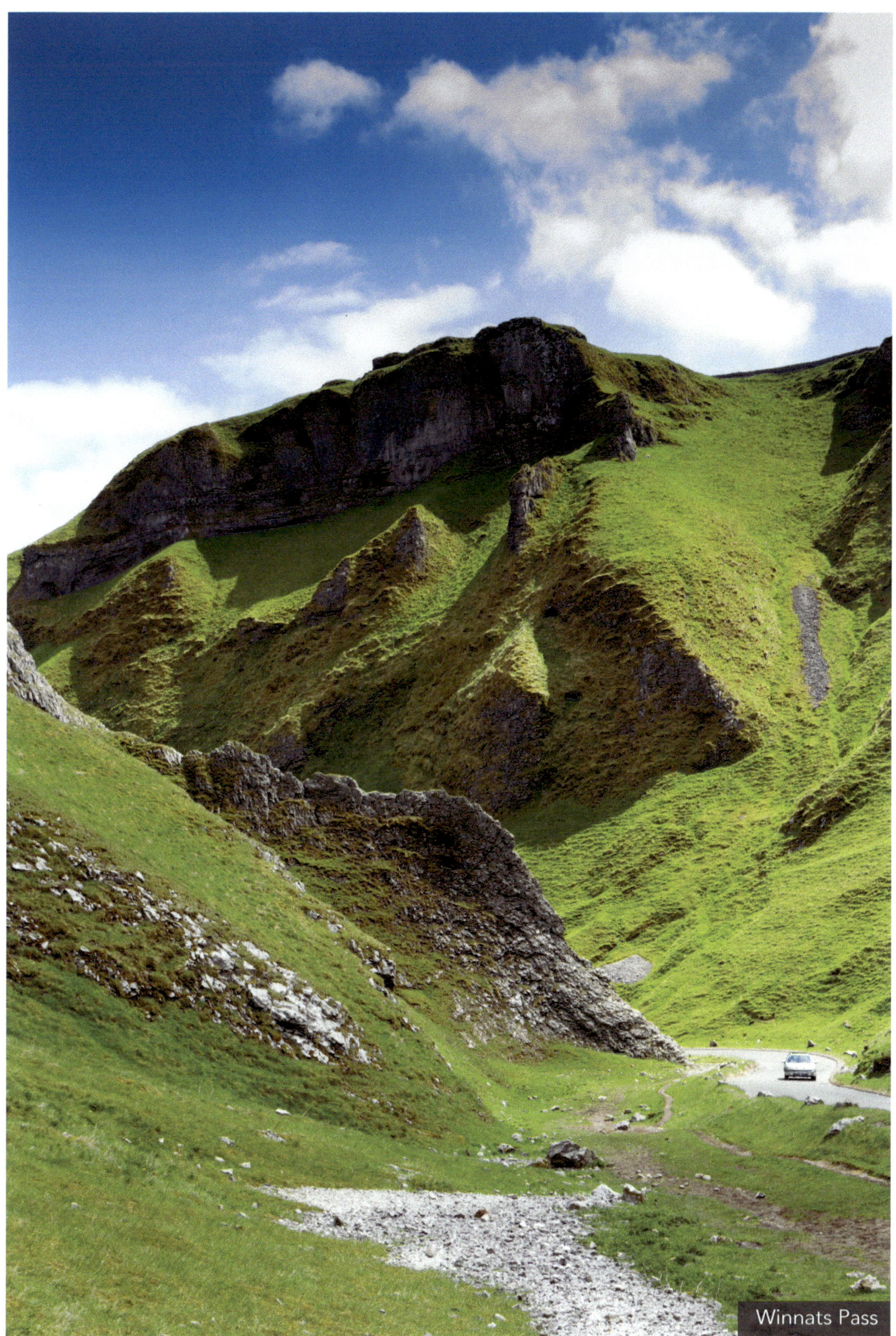

Winnats Pass

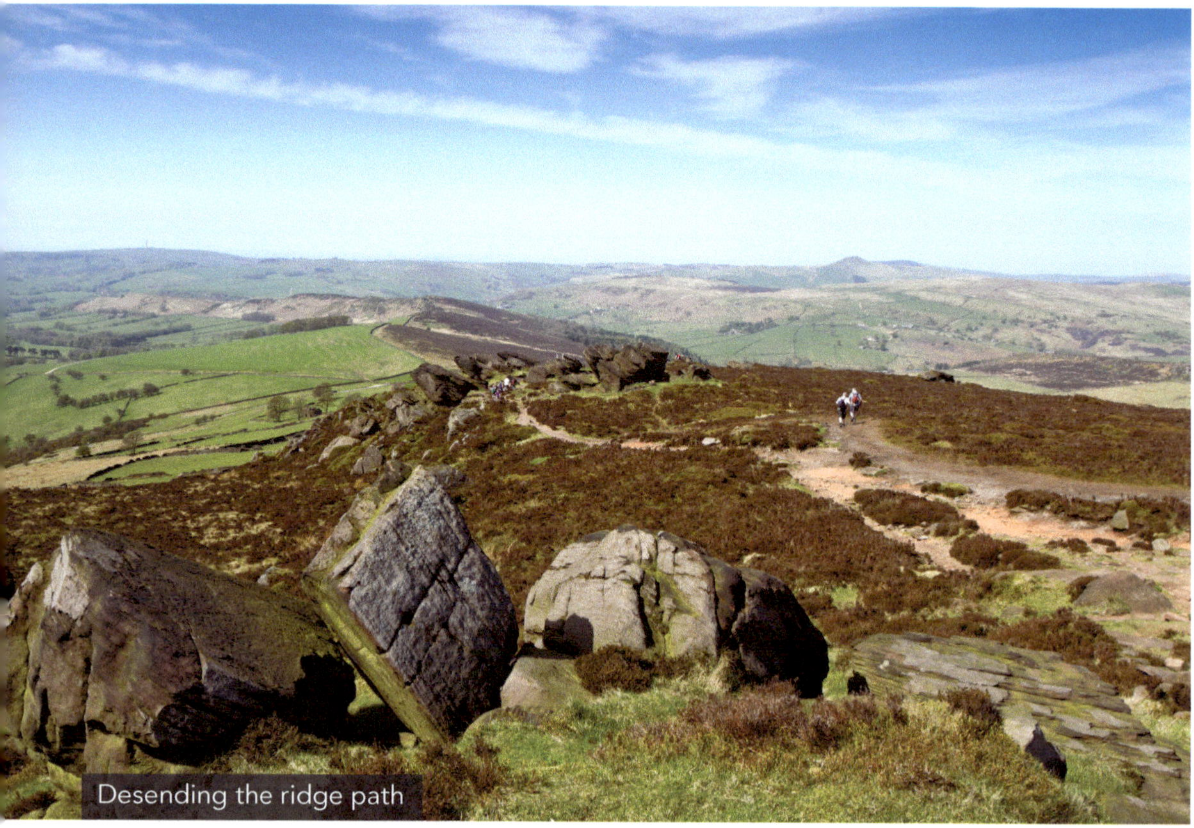

Desending the ridge path

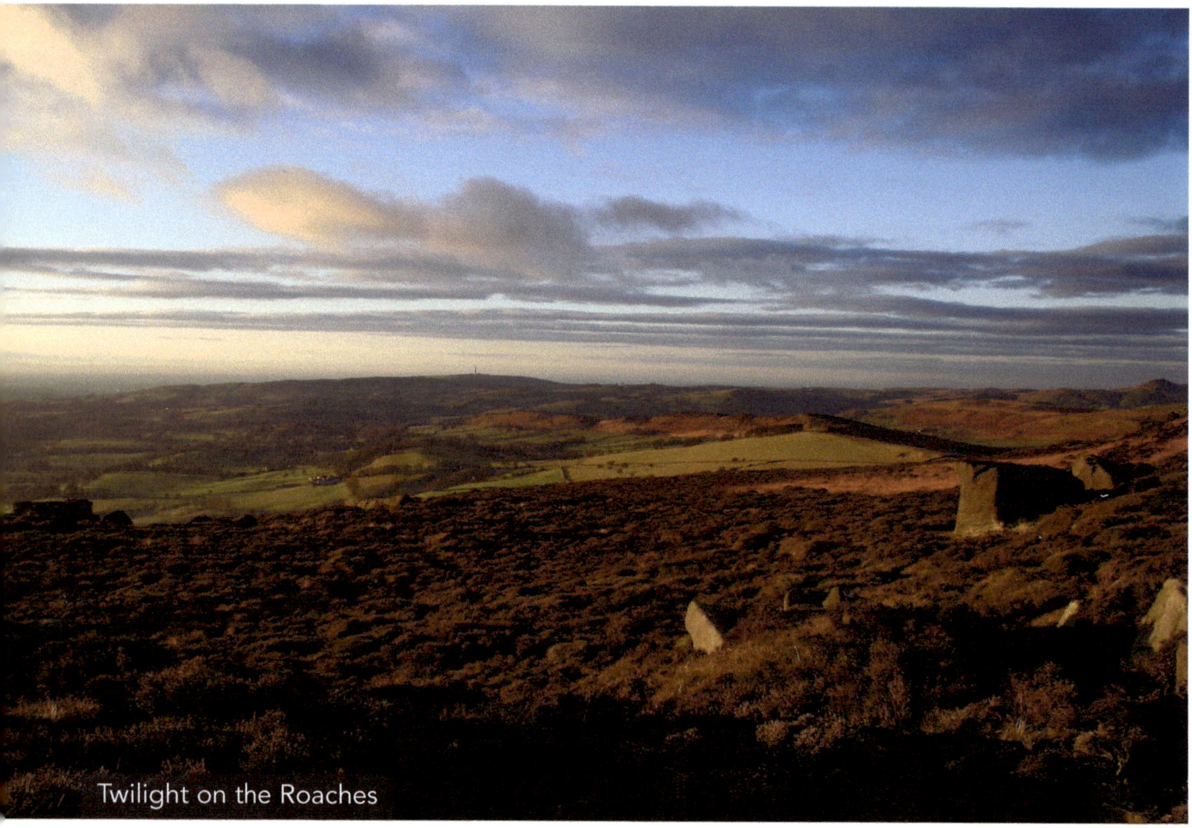

Twilight on the Roaches

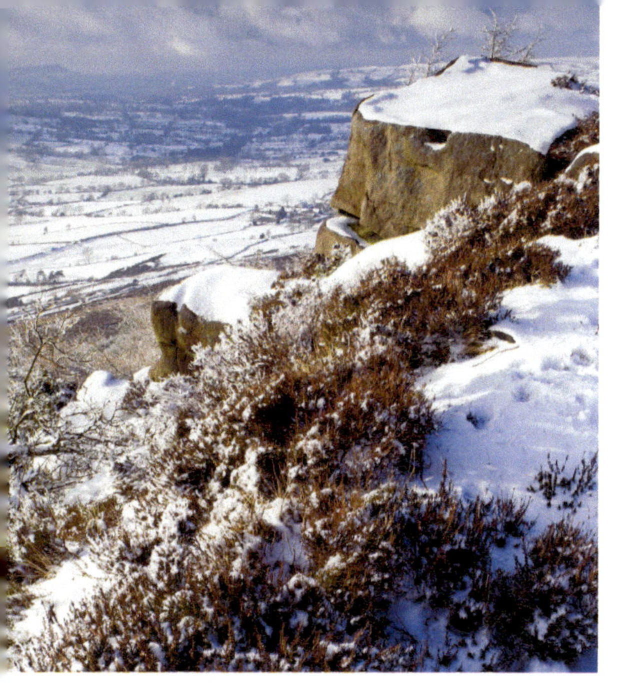

The Roaches

The dramatic, craggy landscape of the Roaches form a gritstone escarpment that is a veritable paradise for hikers and rock climbers, as well as those who prefer a gentle ramble. On a clear day, the magnificent views from atop the ridges can extend as far as Wales' Mount Snowdon and Winter Hill in Lancashire.

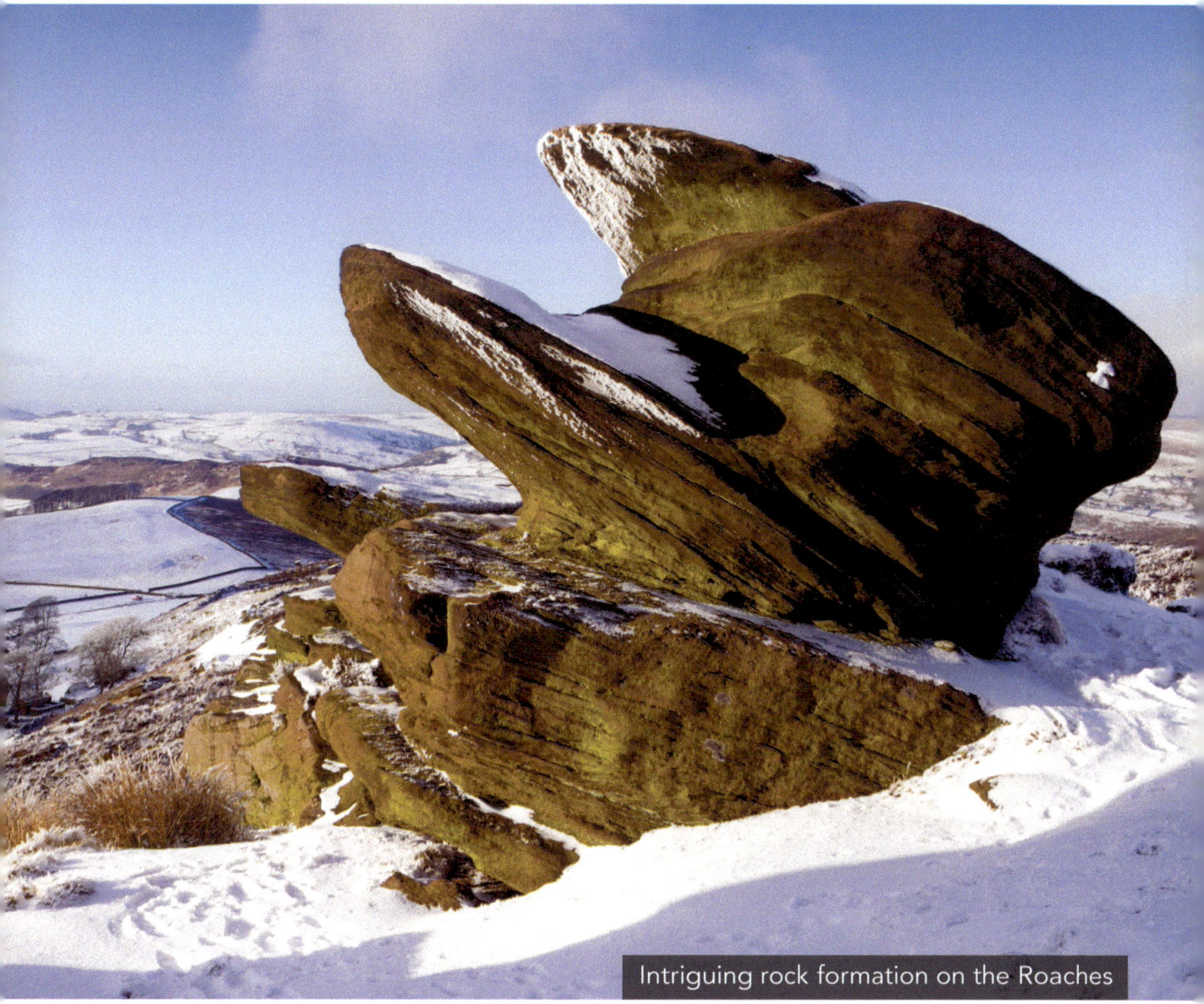

Intriguing rock formation on the Roaches

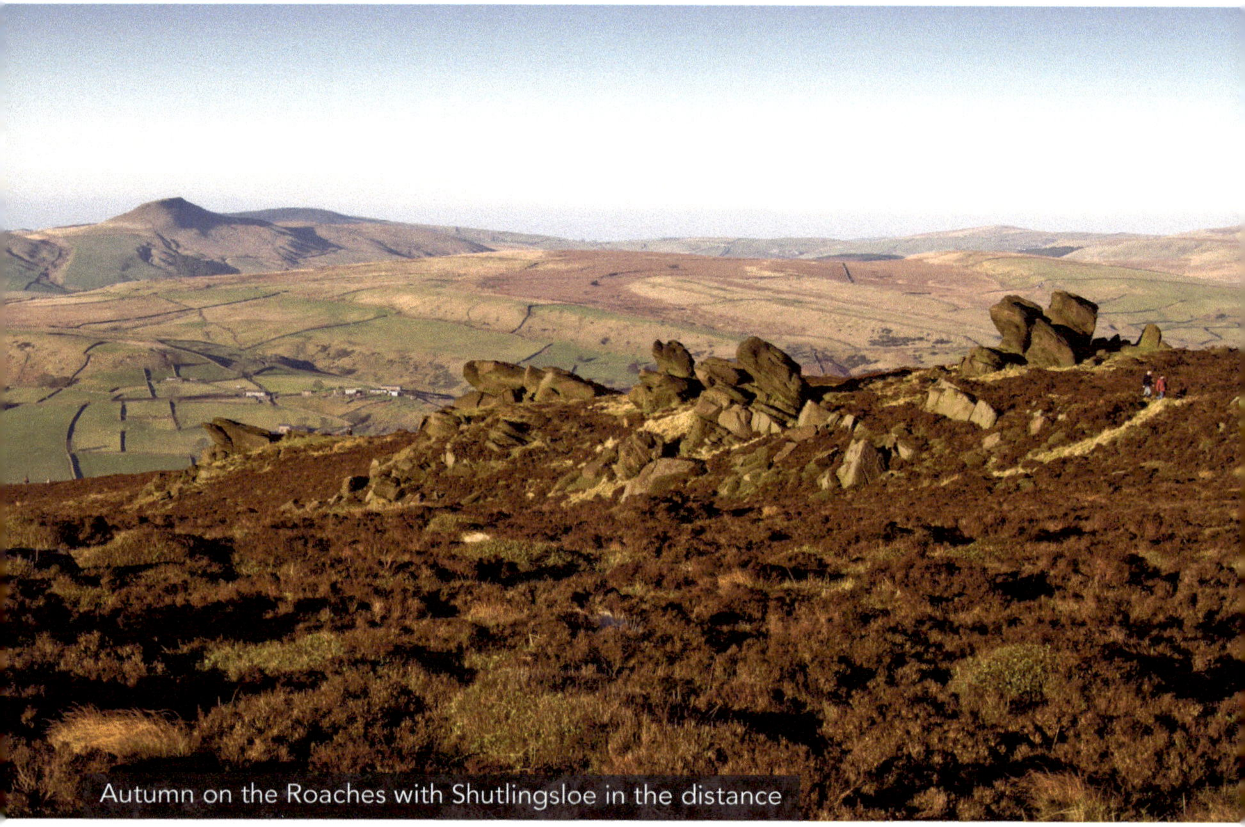

Autumn on the Roaches with Shutlingsloe in the distance

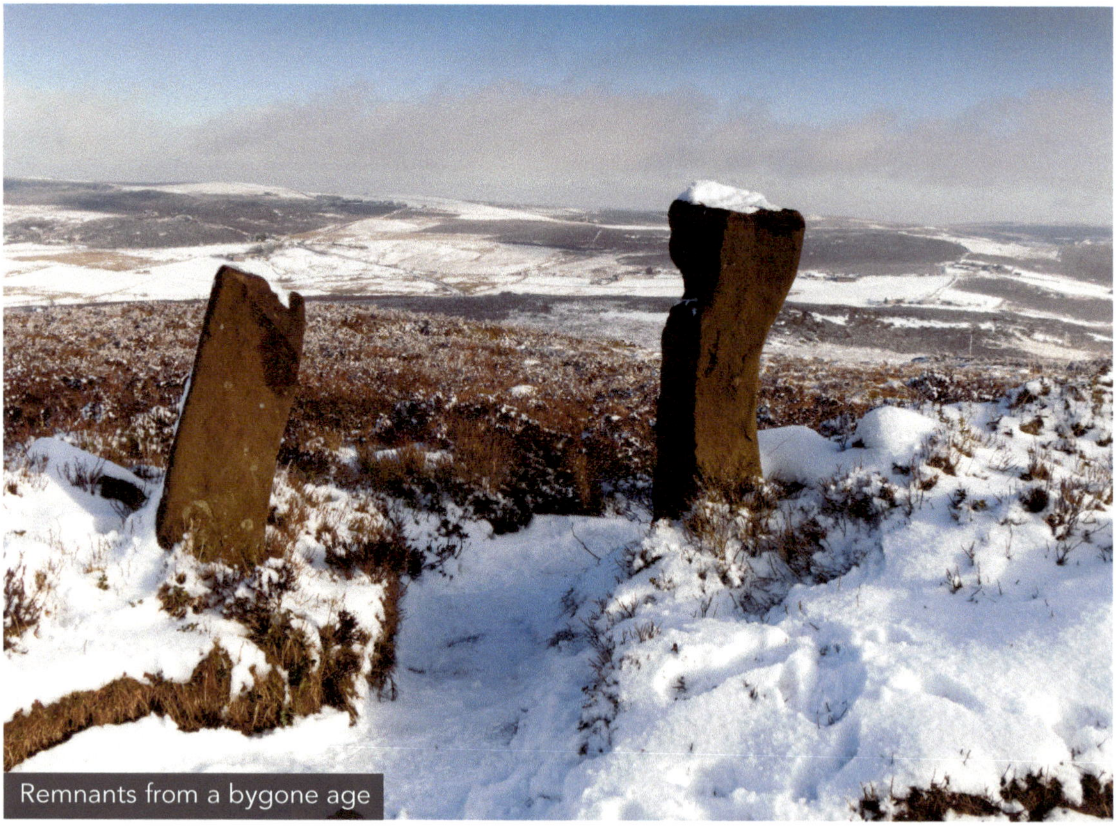

Remnants from a bygone age

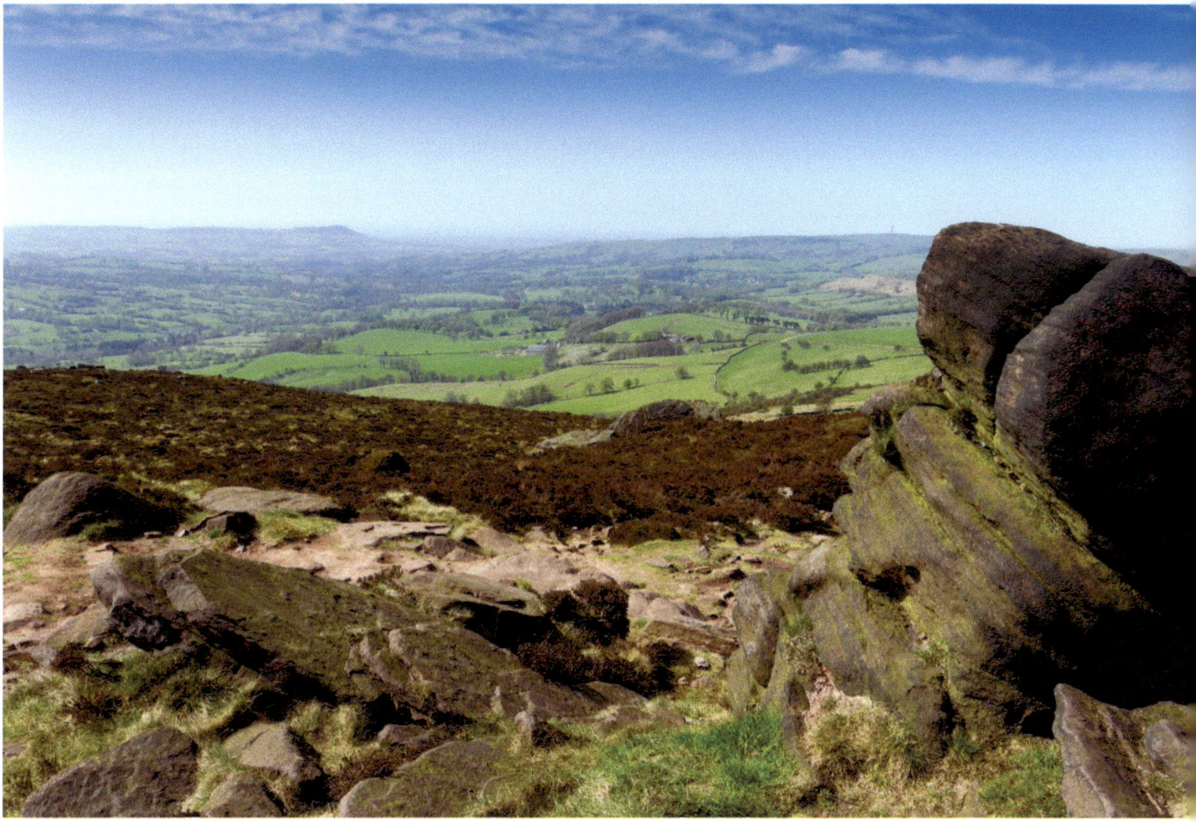

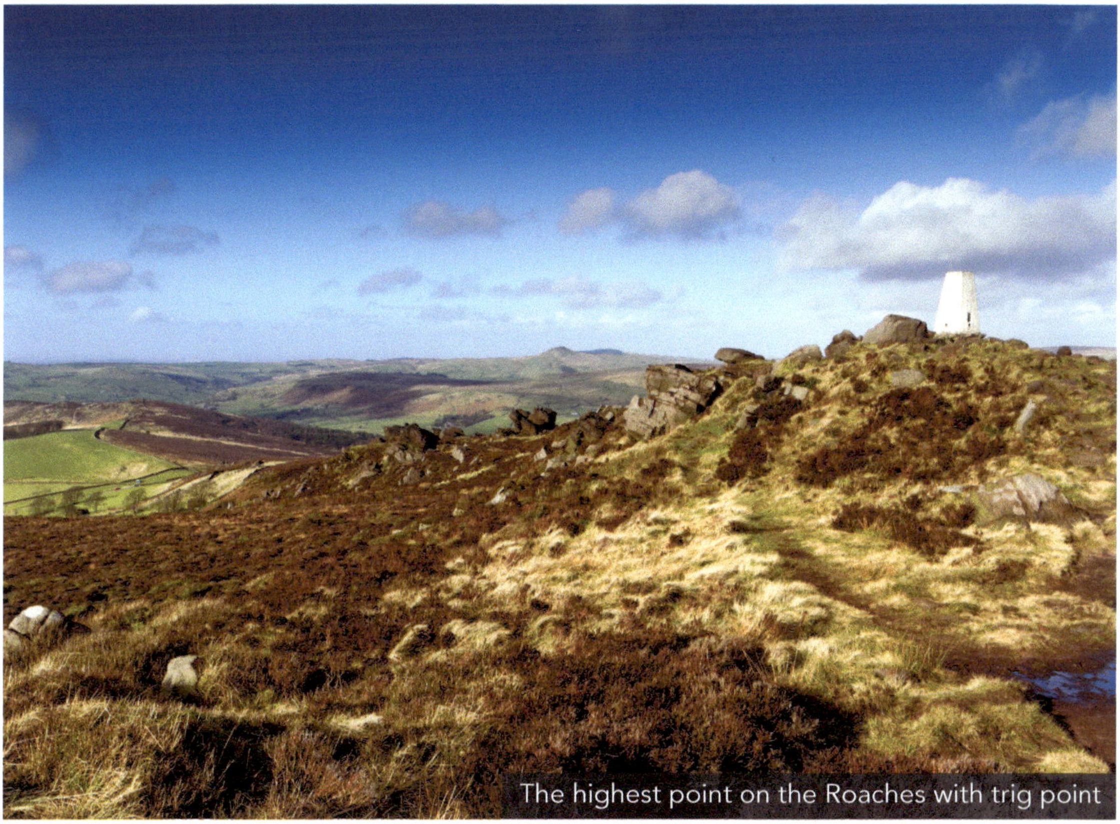

The highest point on the Roaches with trig point

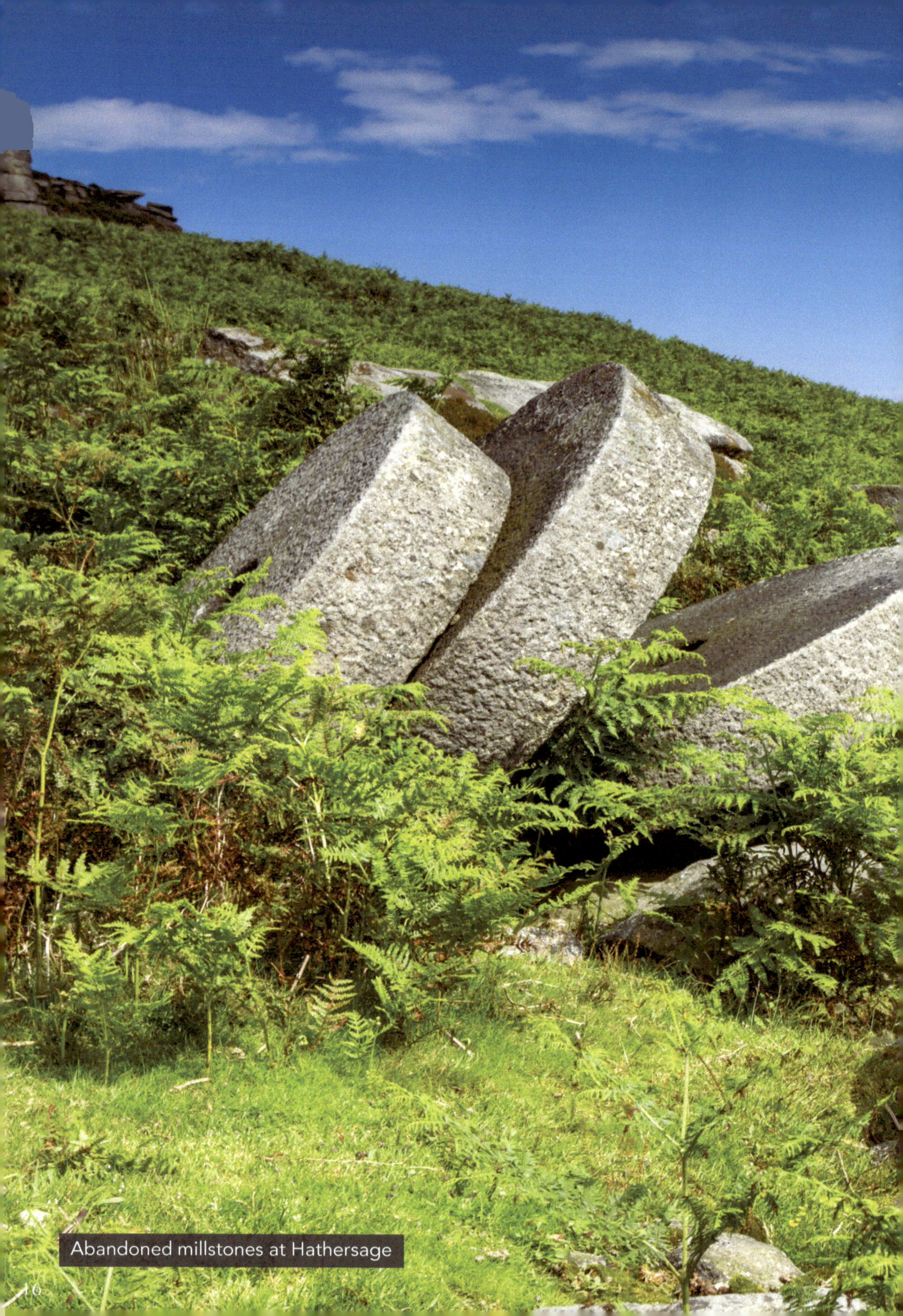

Abandoned millstones at Hathersage

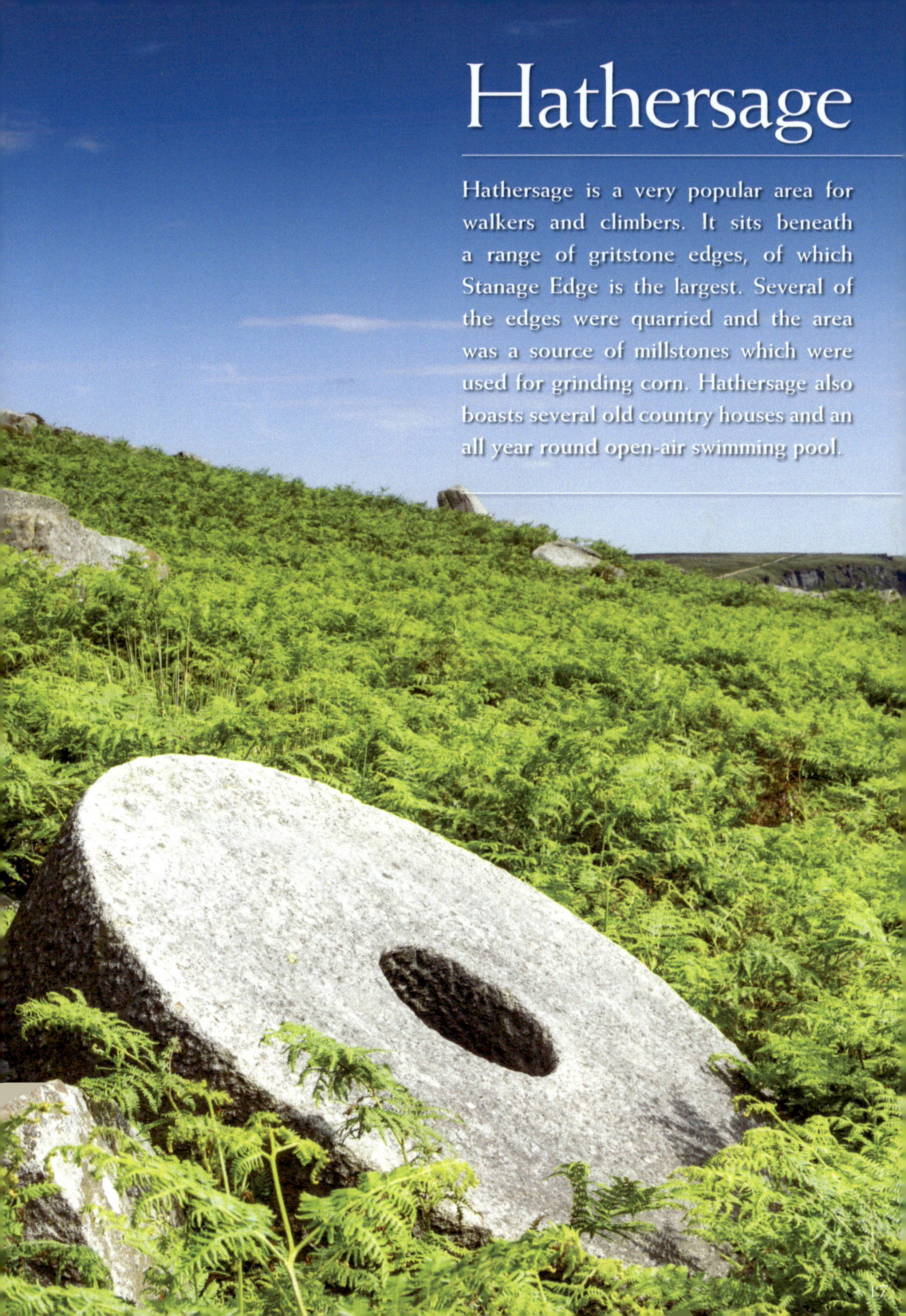

Hathersage

Hathersage is a very popular area for walkers and climbers. It sits beneath a range of gritstone edges, of which Stanage Edge is the largest. Several of the edges were quarried and the area was a source of millstones which were used for grinding corn. Hathersage also boasts several old country houses and an all year round open-air swimming pool.

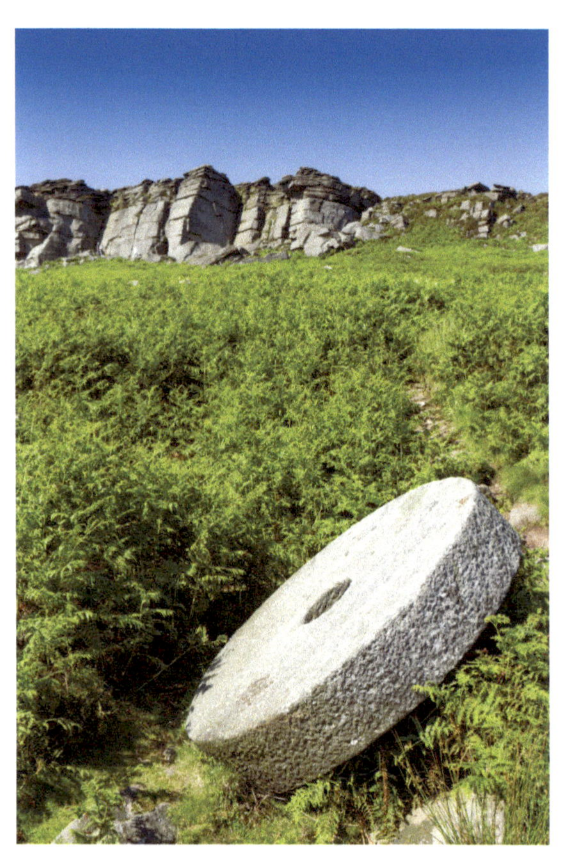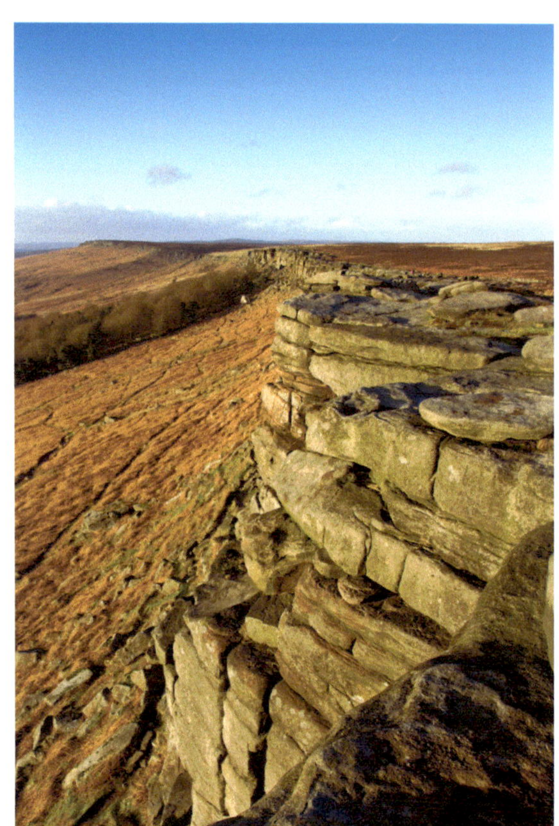

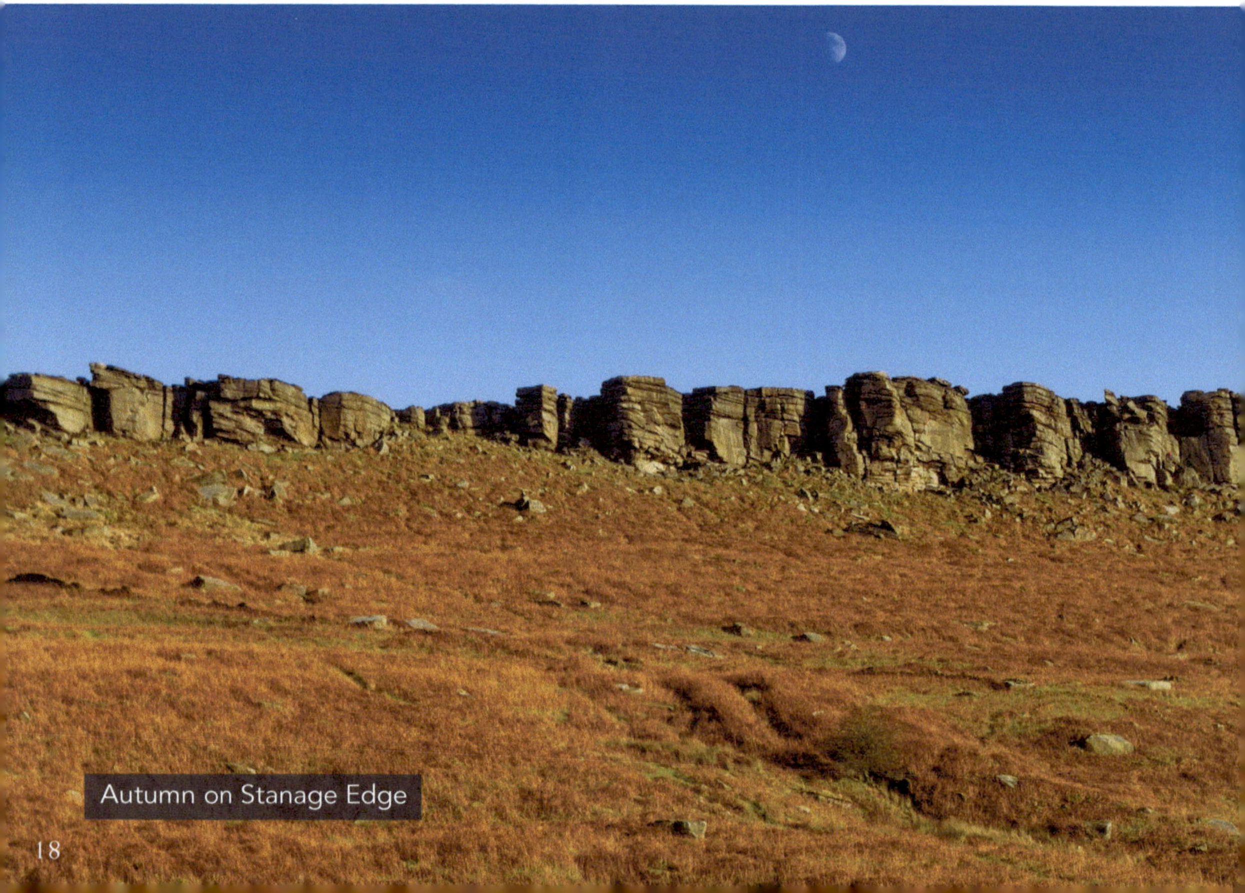

Autumn on Stanage Edge

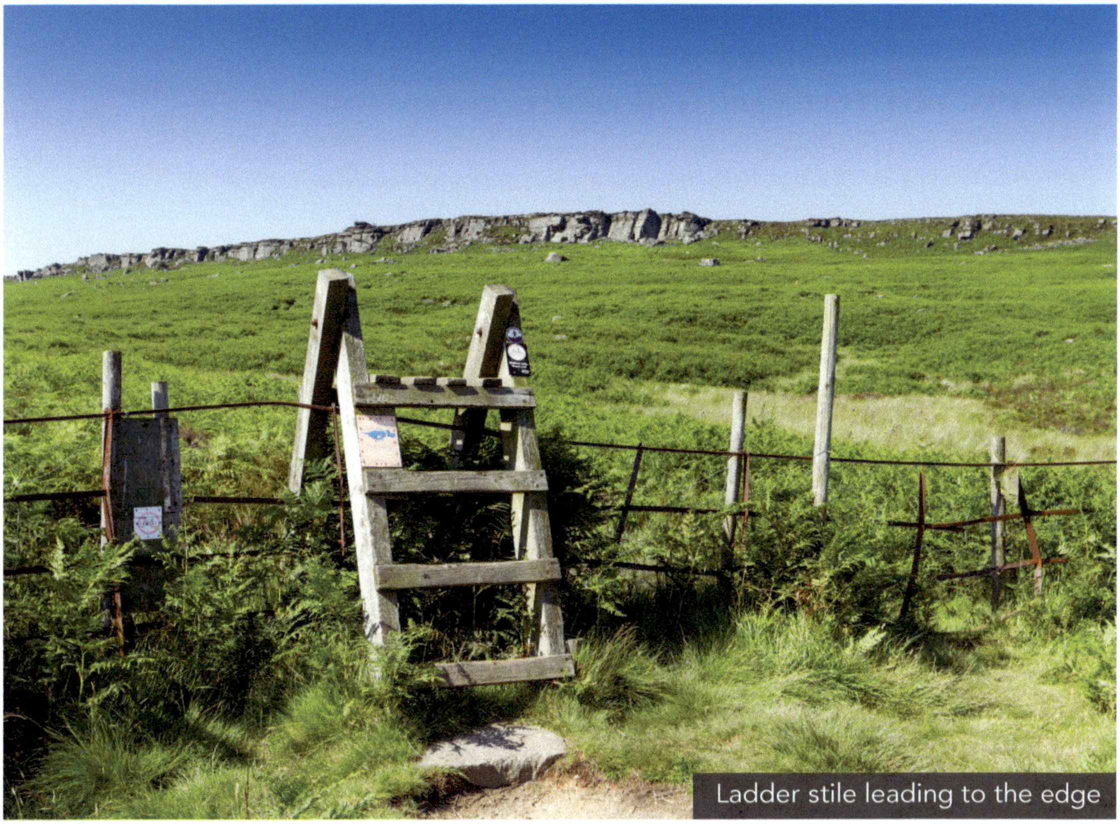

Ladder stile leading to the edge

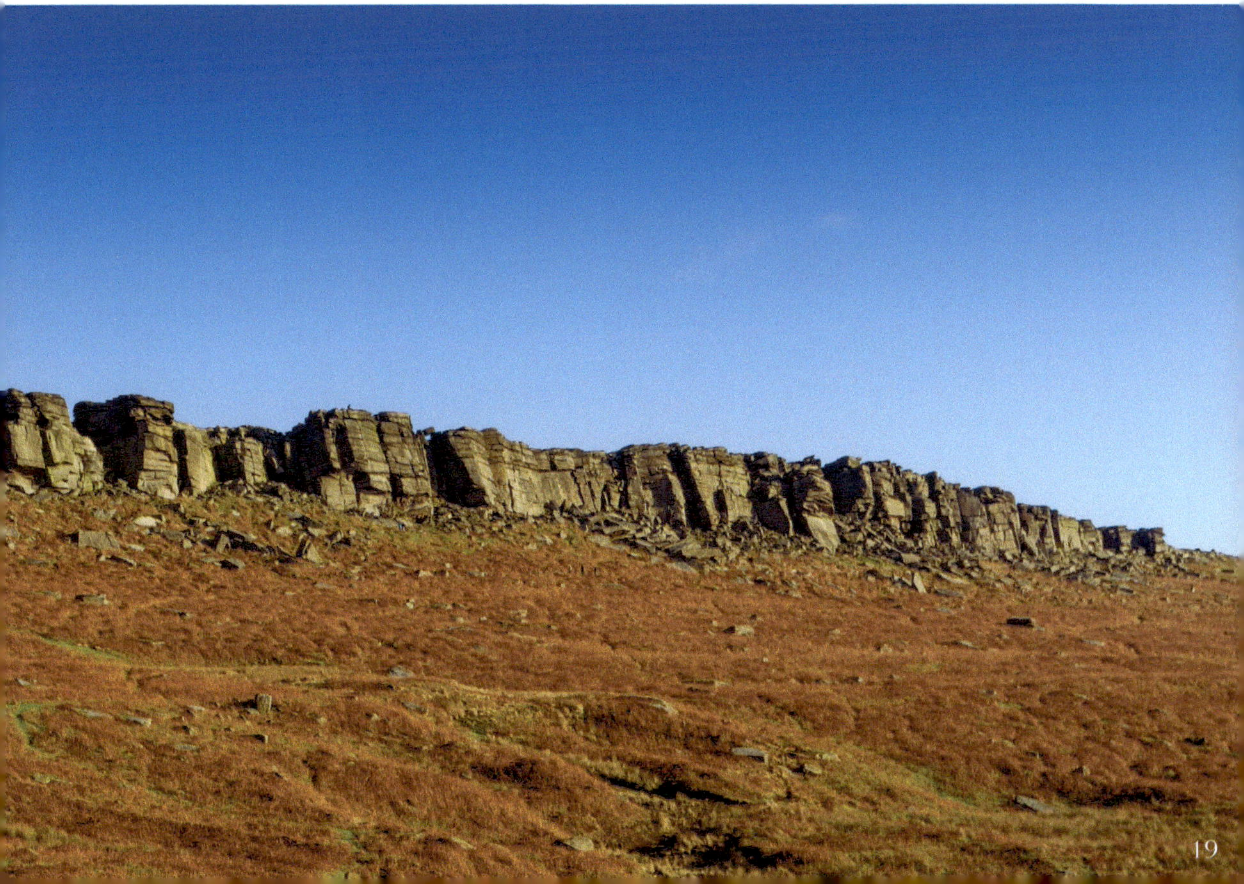

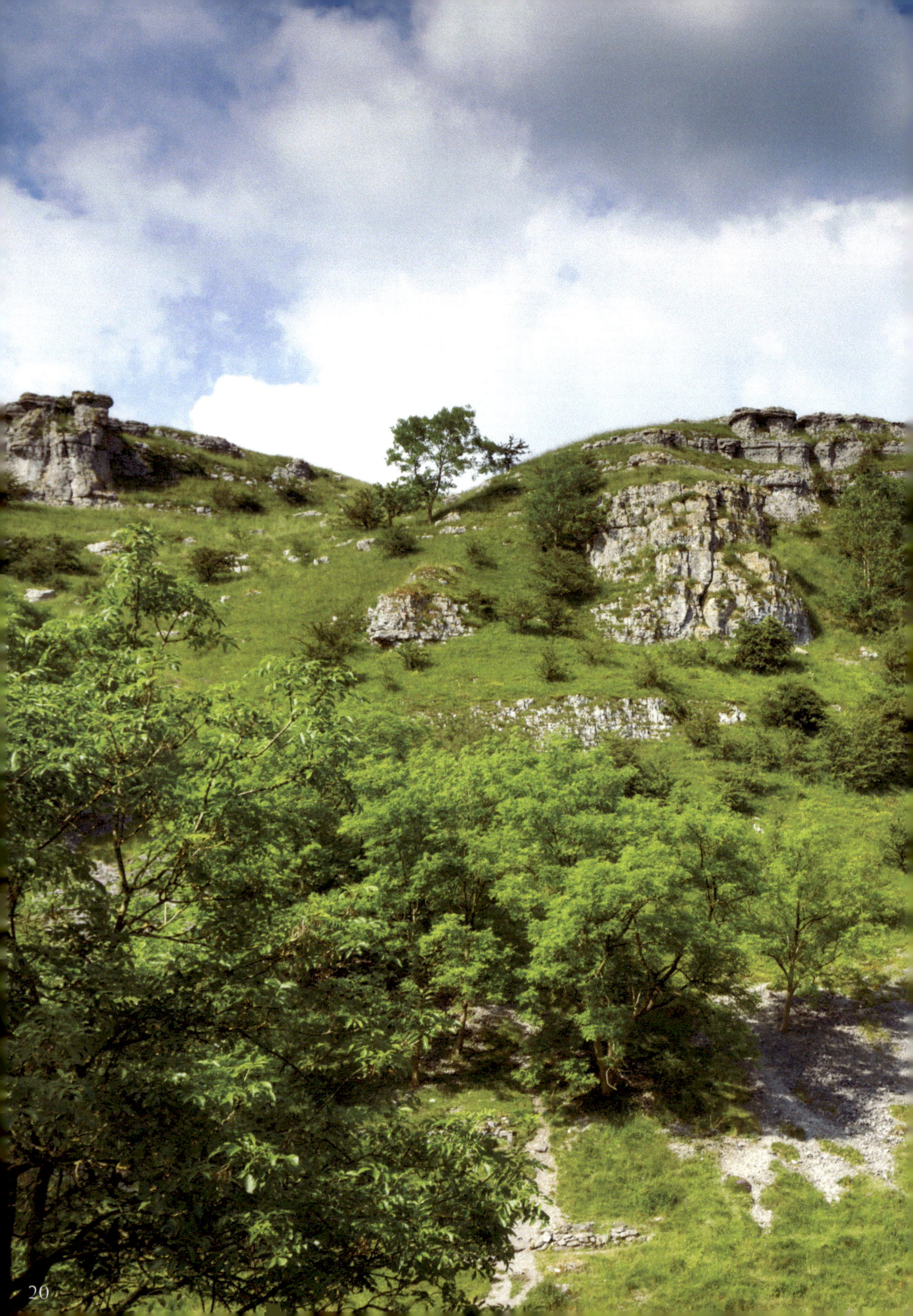

Lathkill Dale

Lathkill Dale is considered one of the Peak District's finest walks for its fabulous greenery and tranquil atmosphere. The trail runs alongside the River Lathkill, known for its crystal clear waters. The ruins of a 19th century lead mine can be seen on the north side of the valley.

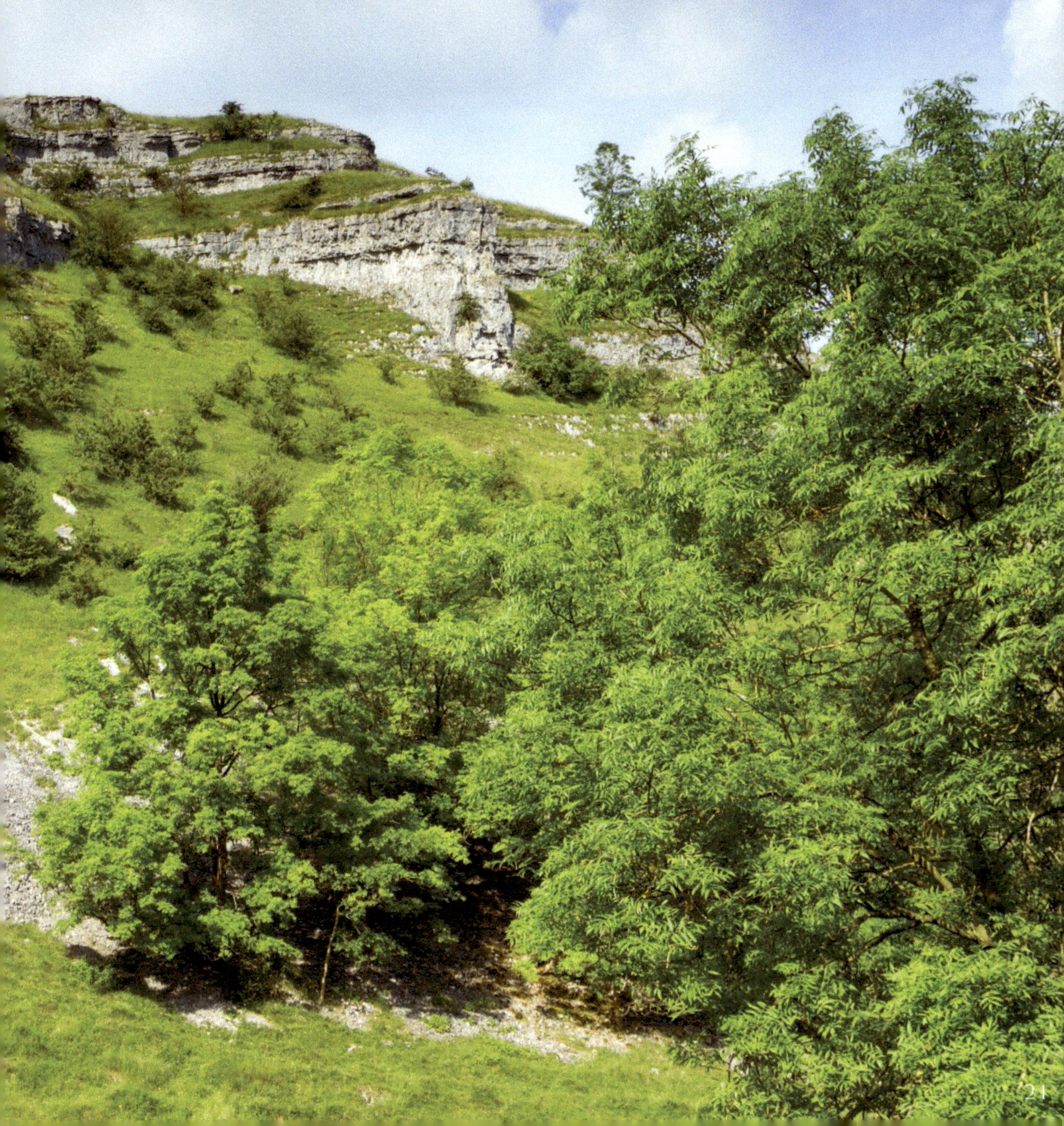

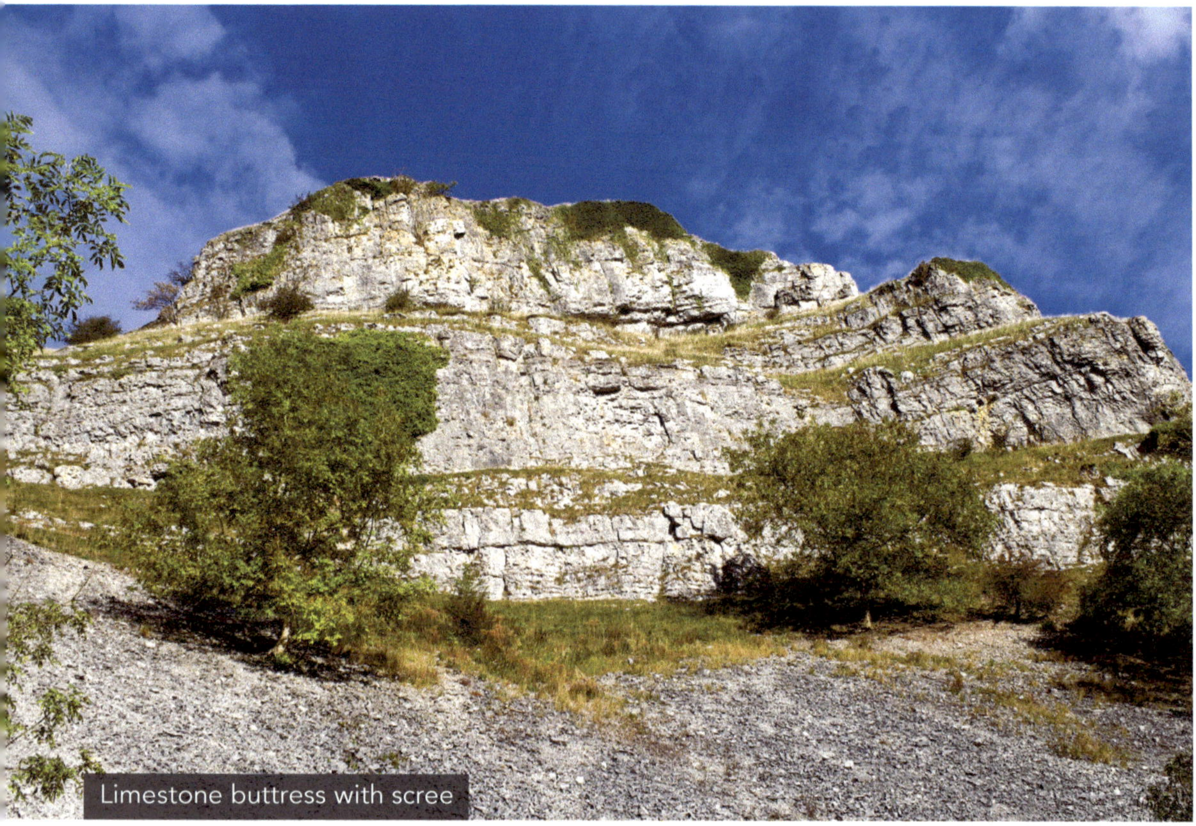

Limestone buttress with scree

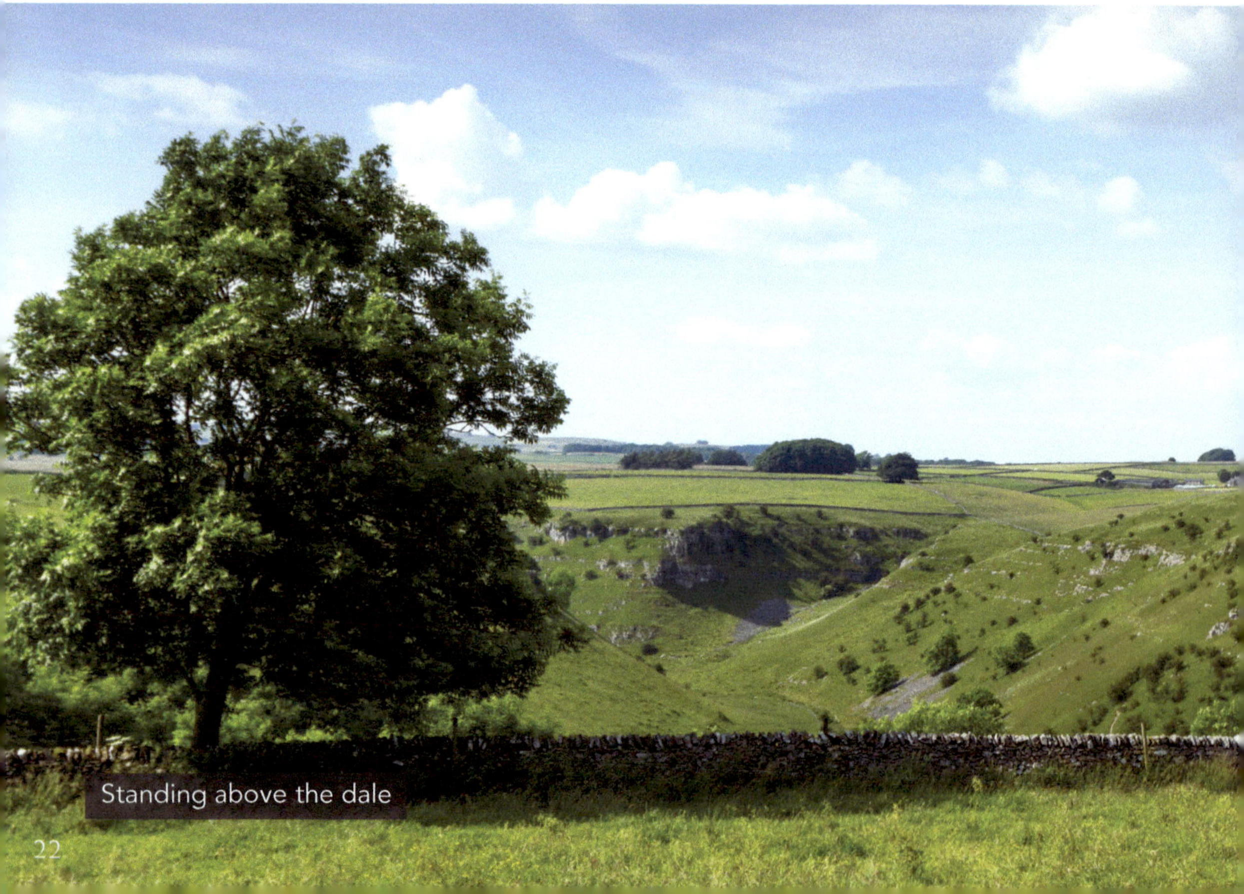

Standing above the dale

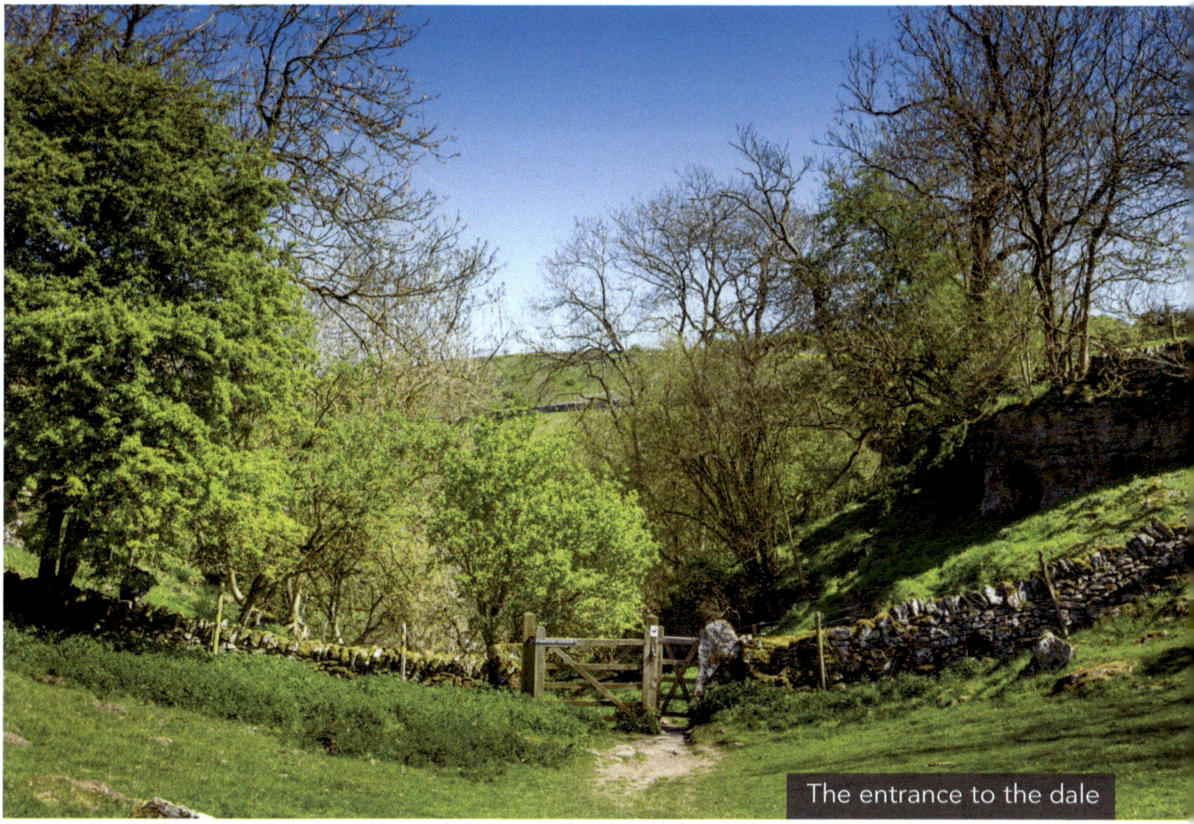

The entrance to the dale

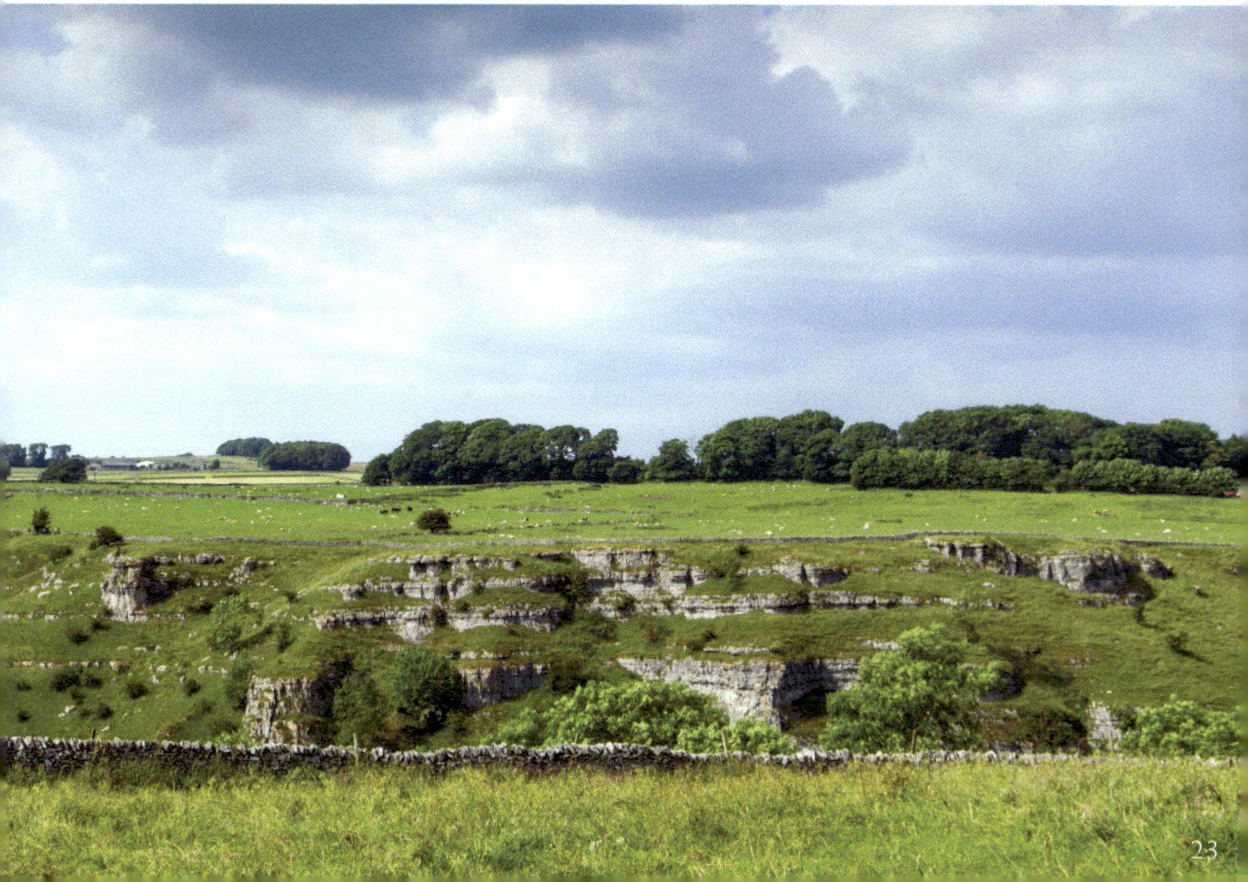

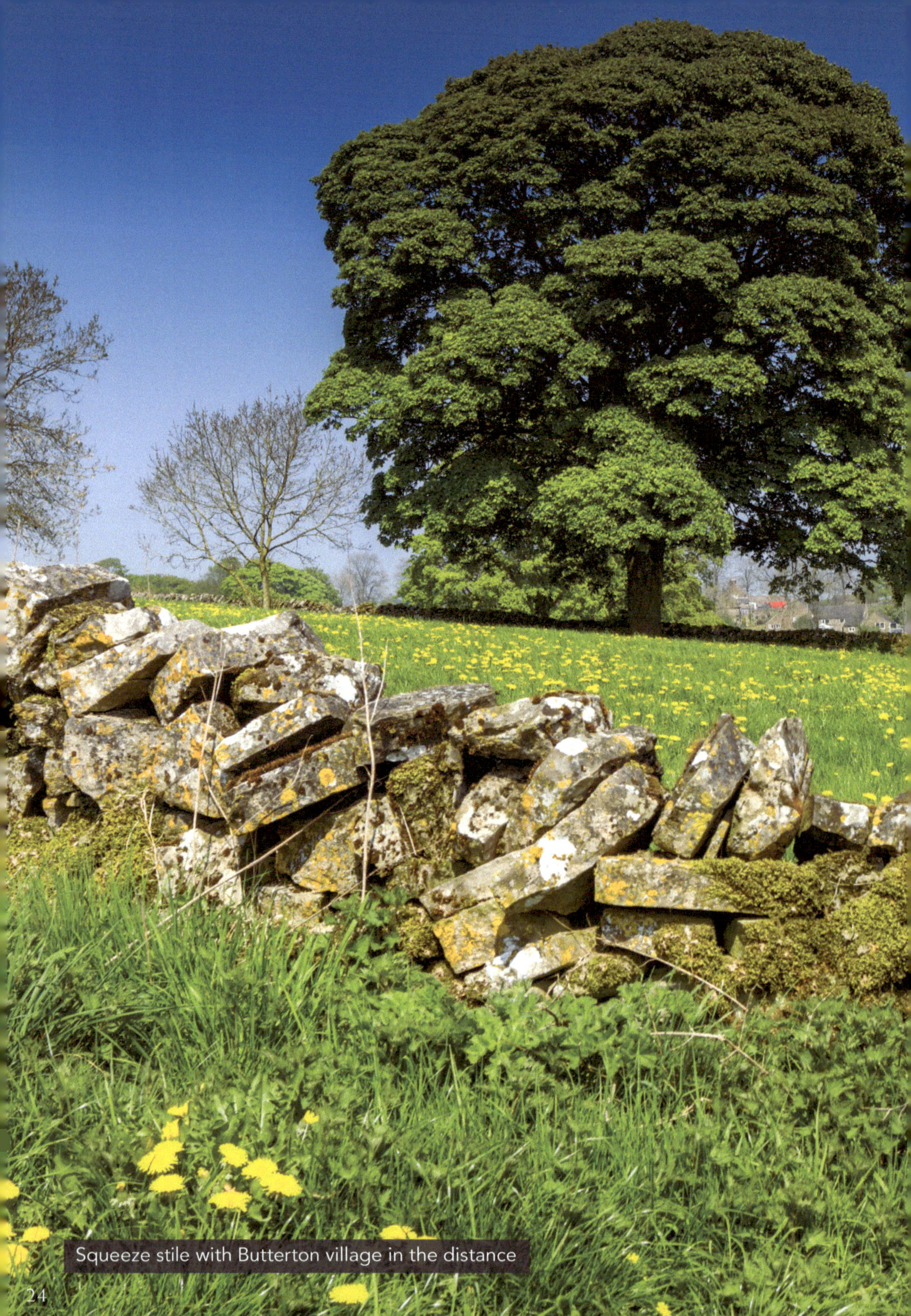

Squeeze stile with Butterton village in the distance

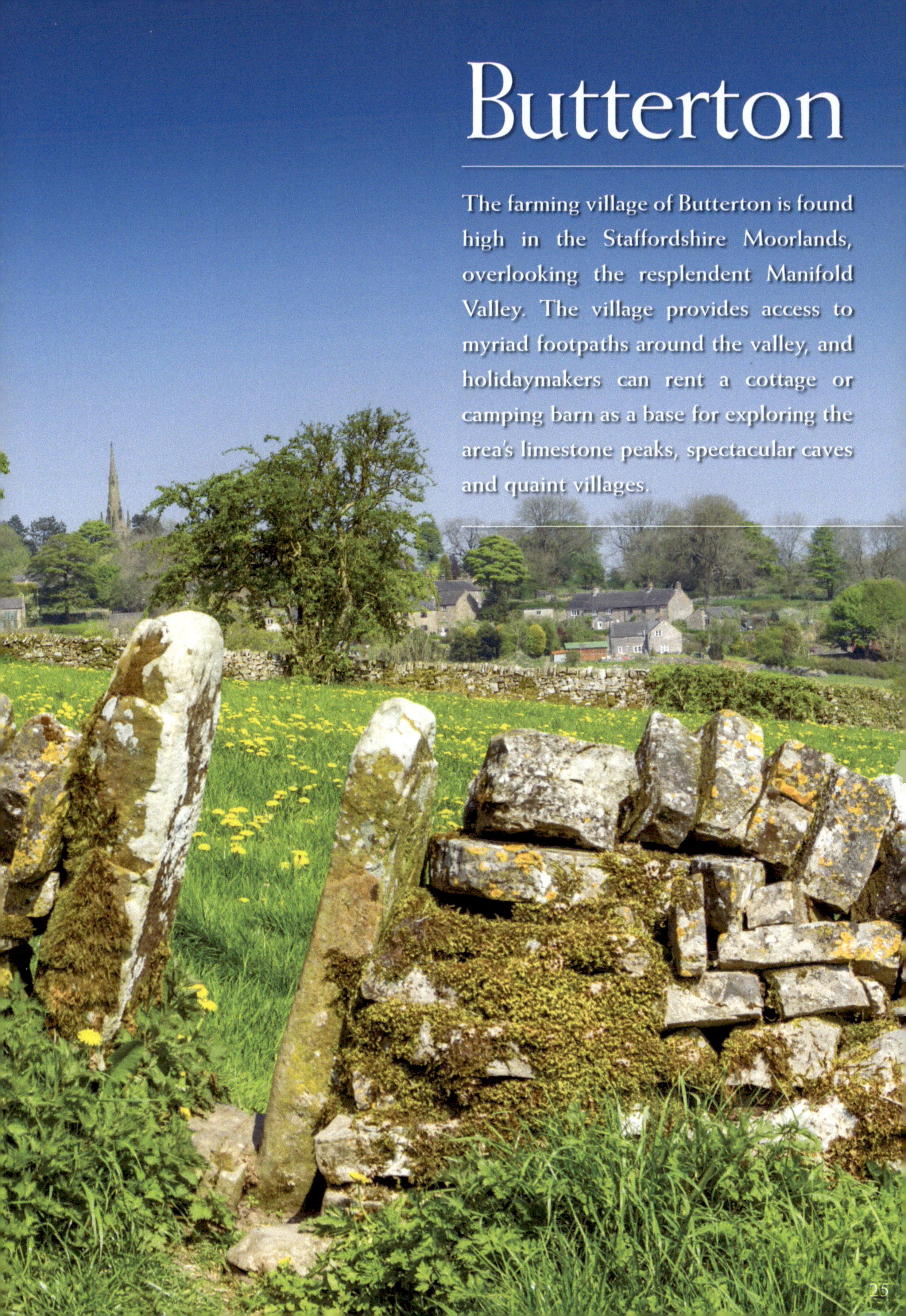

Butterton

The farming village of Butterton is found high in the Staffordshire Moorlands, overlooking the resplendent Manifold Valley. The village provides access to myriad footpaths around the valley, and holidaymakers can rent a cottage or camping barn as a base for exploring the area's limestone peaks, spectacular caves and quaint villages.

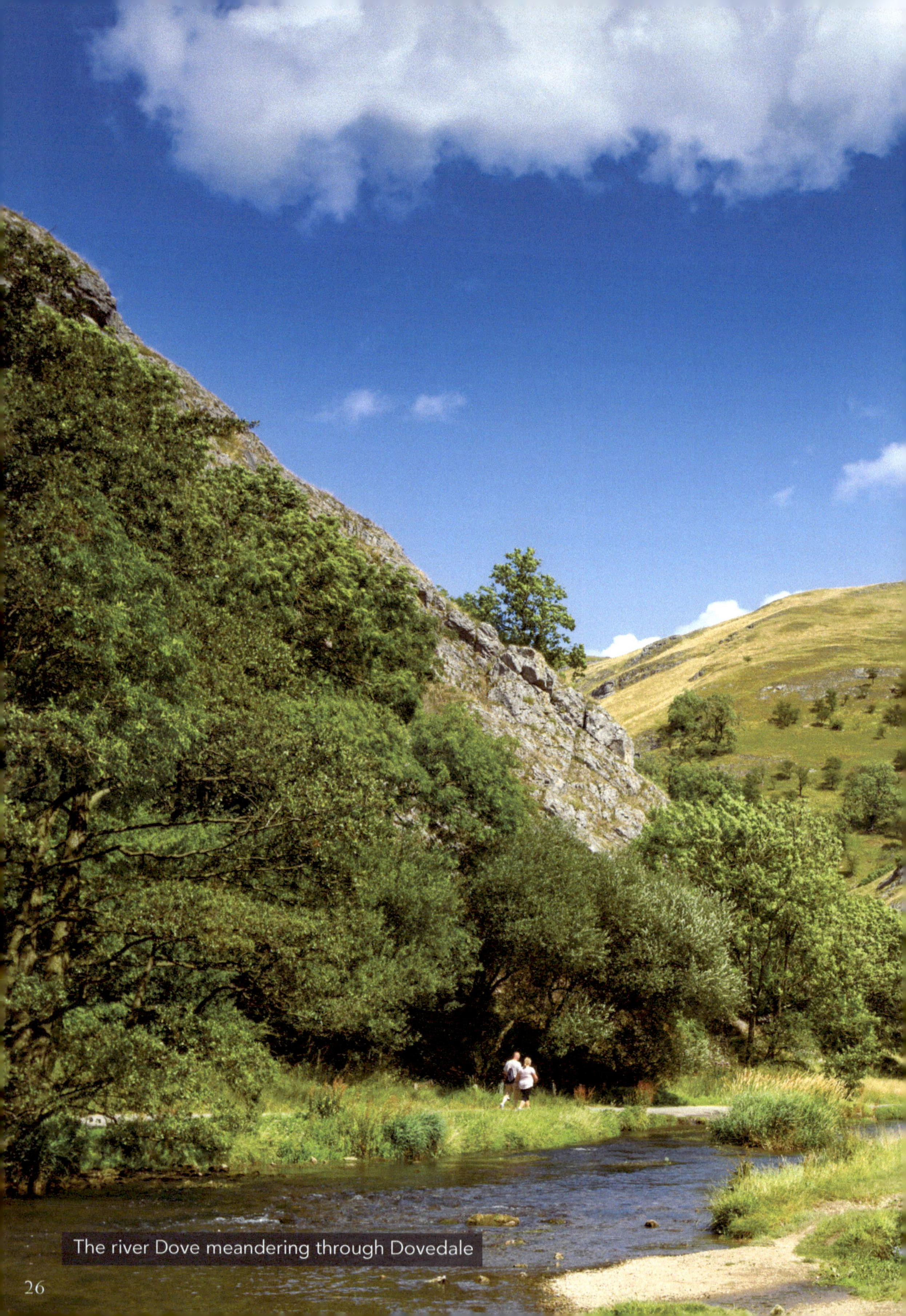

The river Dove meandering through Dovedale

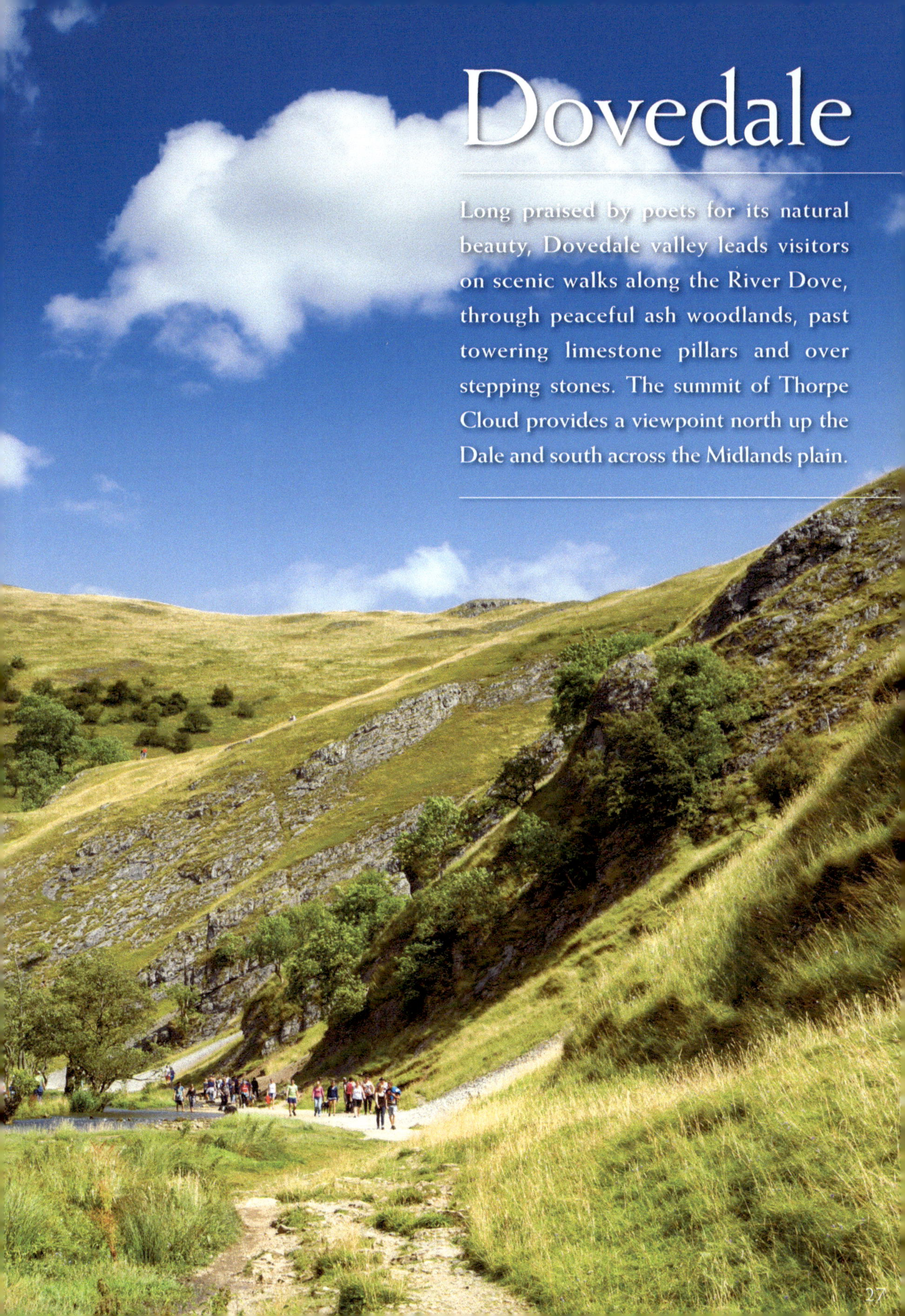

Dovedale

Long praised by poets for its natural beauty, Dovedale valley leads visitors on scenic walks along the River Dove, through peaceful ash woodlands, past towering limestone pillars and over stepping stones. The summit of Thorpe Cloud provides a viewpoint north up the Dale and south across the Midlands plain.

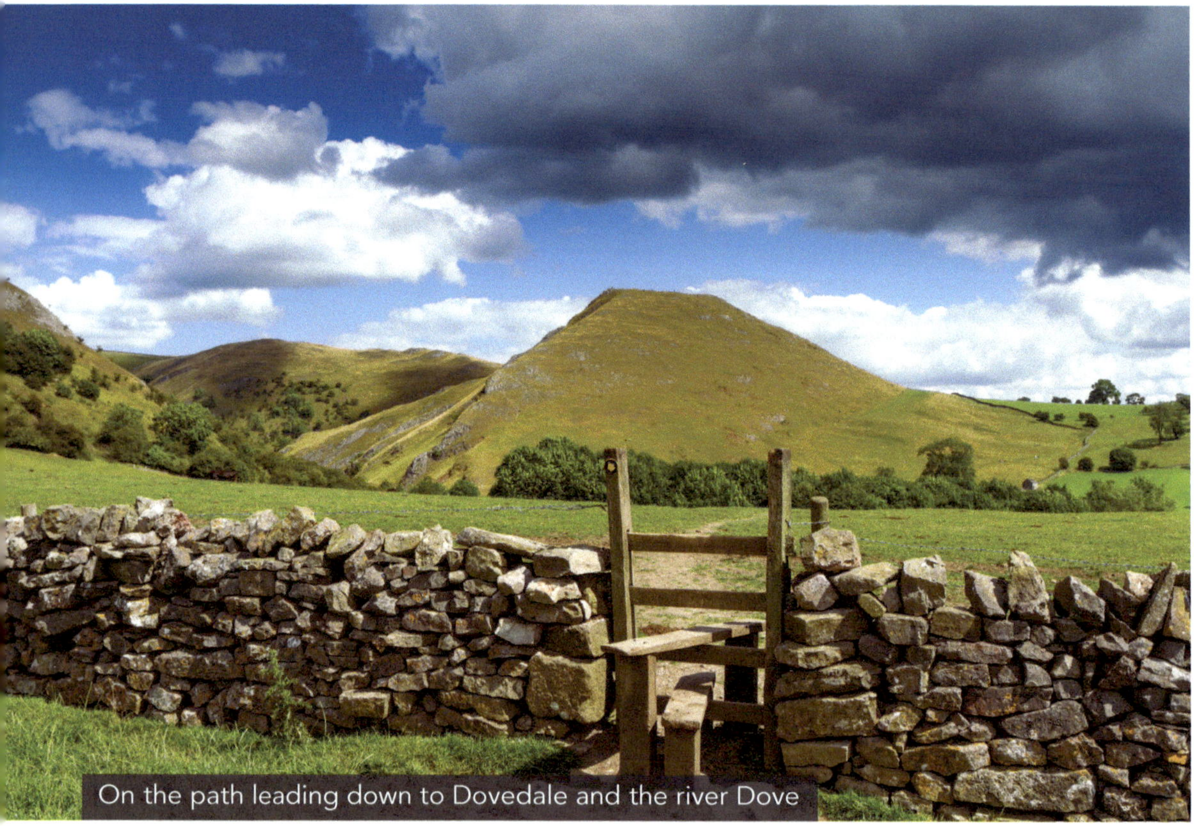

On the path leading down to Dovedale and the river Dove

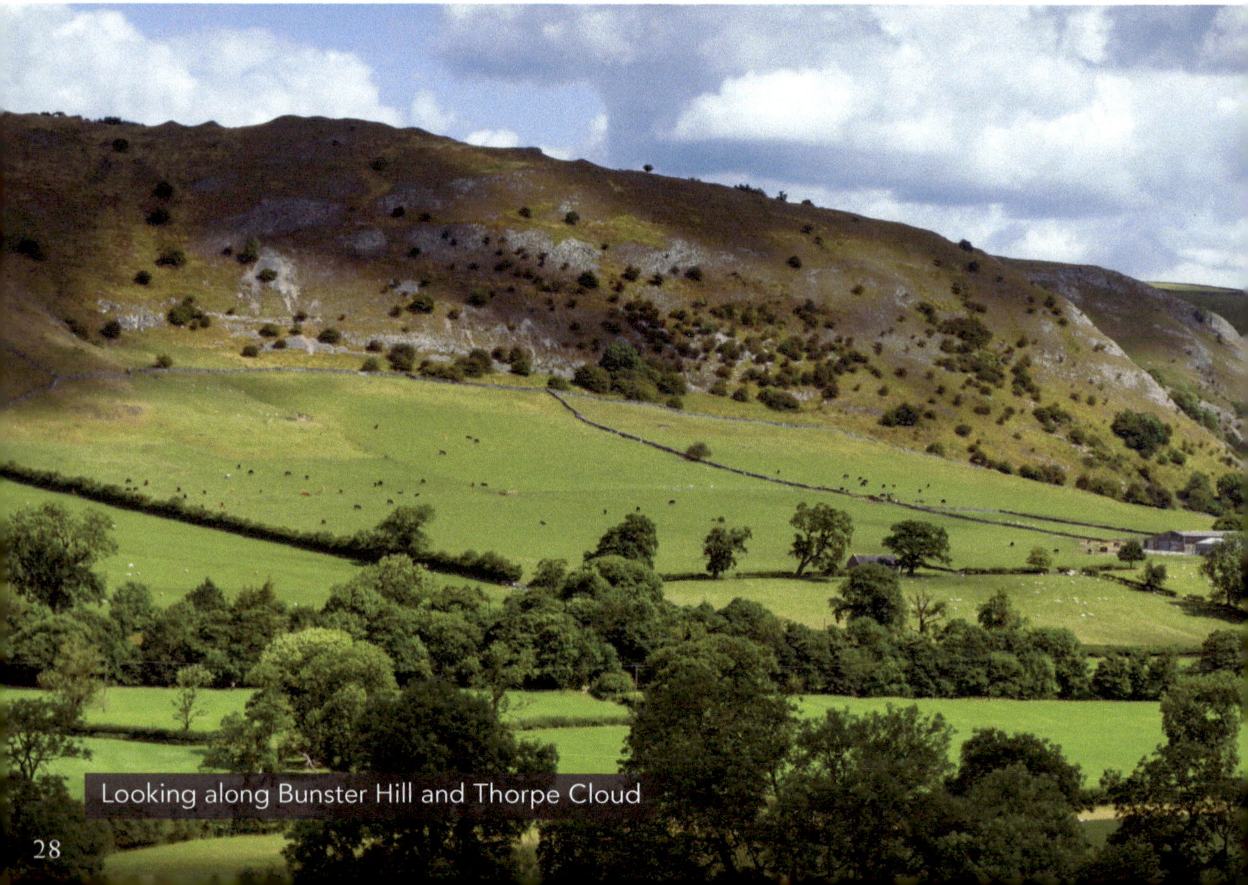

Looking along Bunster Hill and Thorpe Cloud

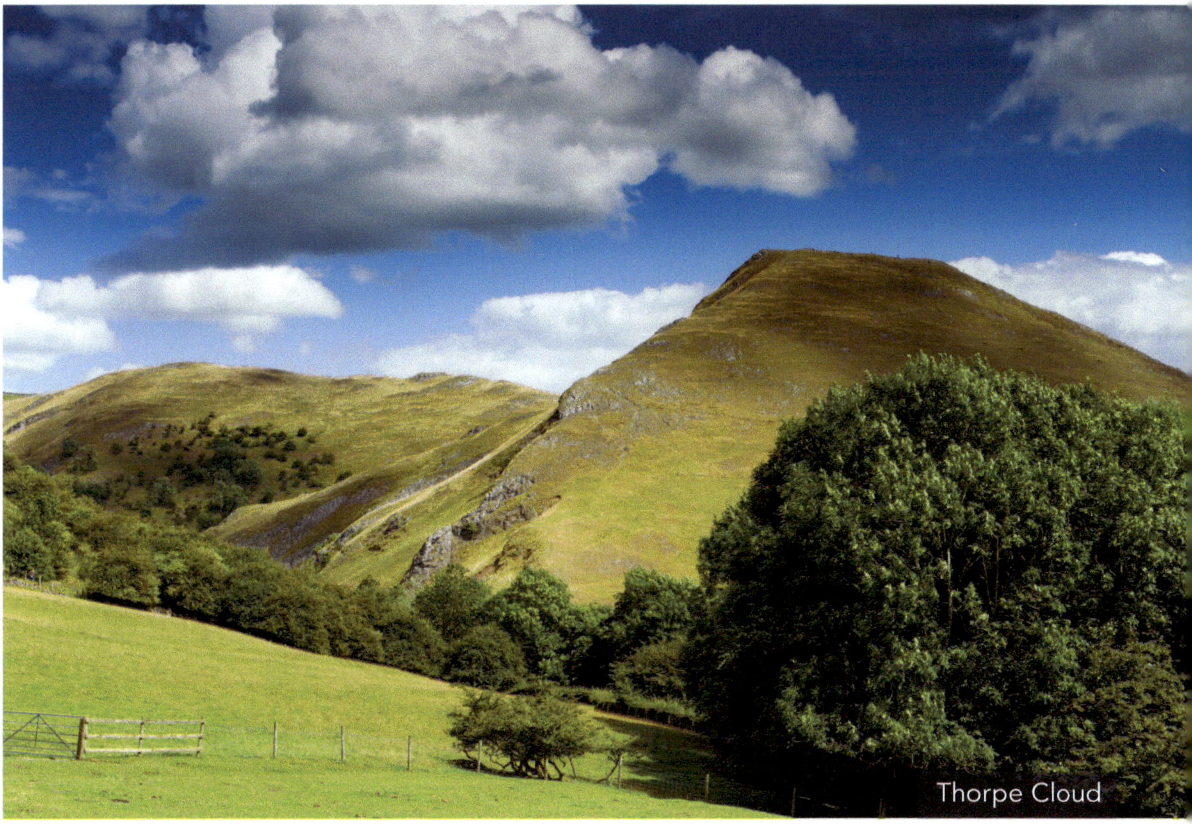

Thorpe Cloud

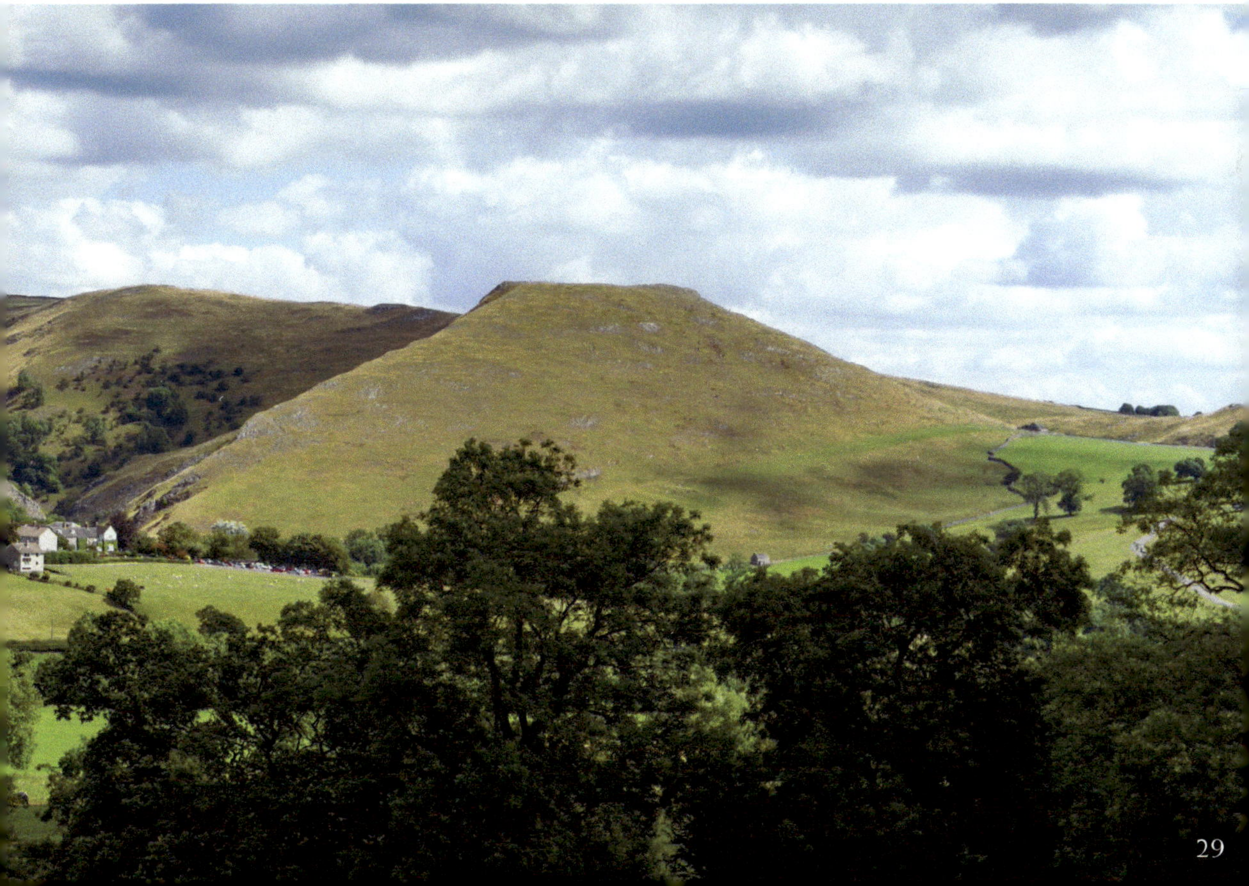

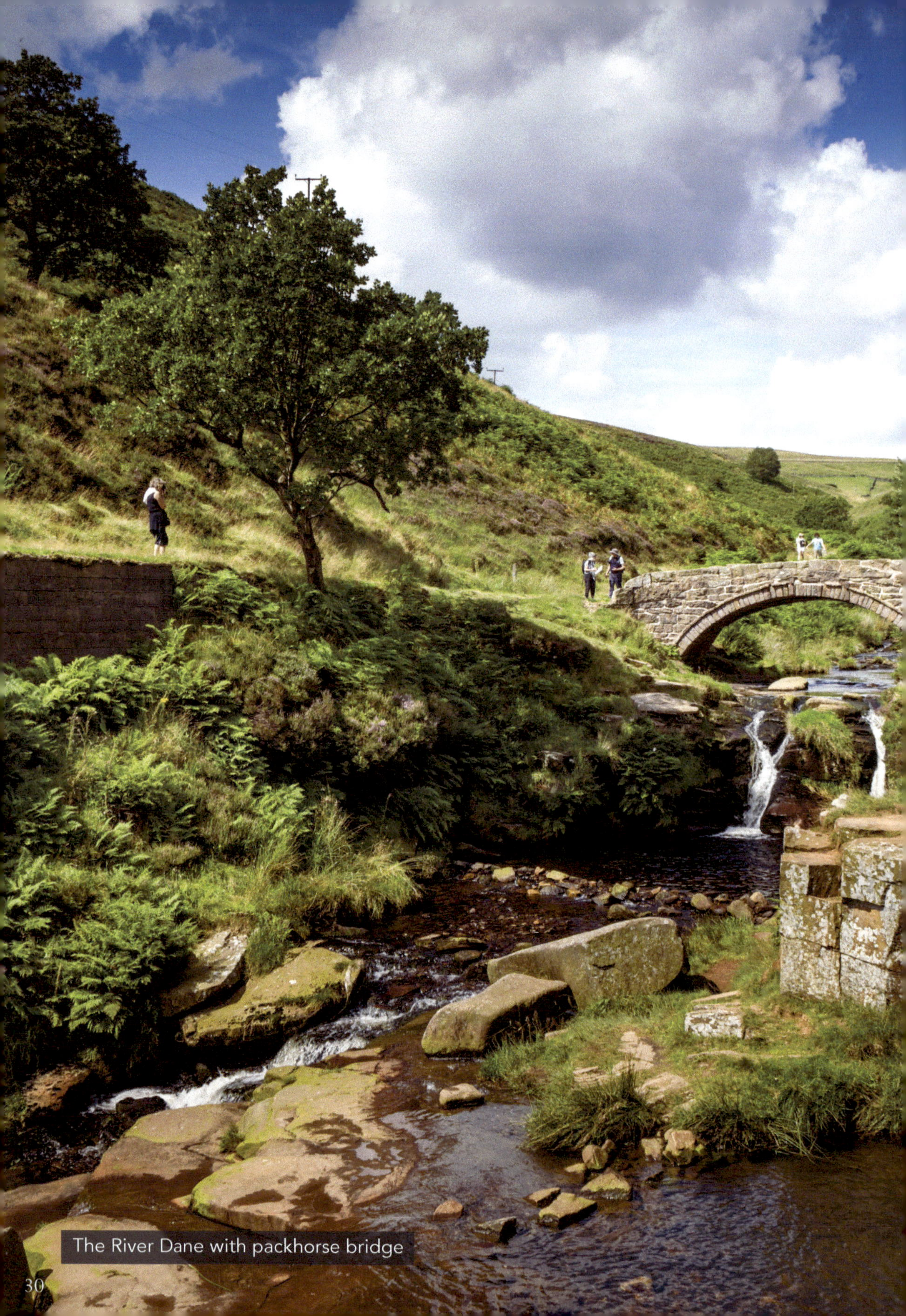

The River Dane with packhorse bridge

Three Shires Head

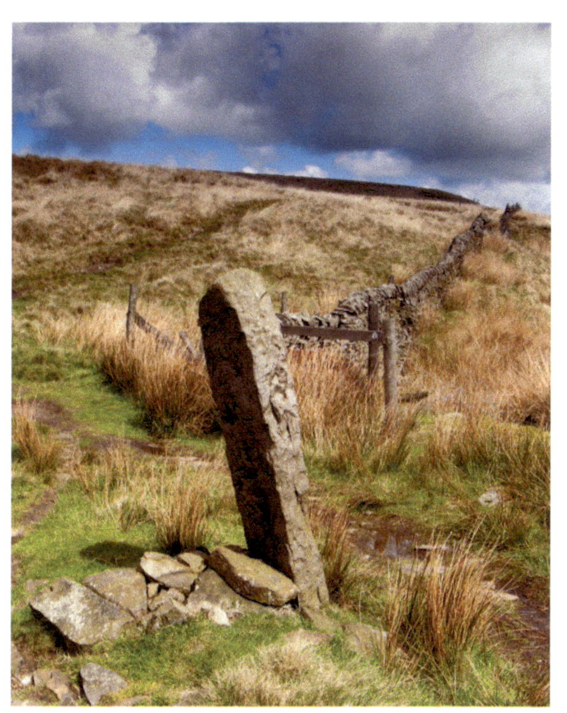

Three Shires Head is the point at which the counties of Cheshire, Derbyshire and Staffordshire meet on Axe Edge Moor. The picturesque packhorse bridge that crosses the River Dane was constructed in the late 18th century and is a favourite landmark, while waterfalls and plunge pools offer a welcome dip after a summer day's walking.

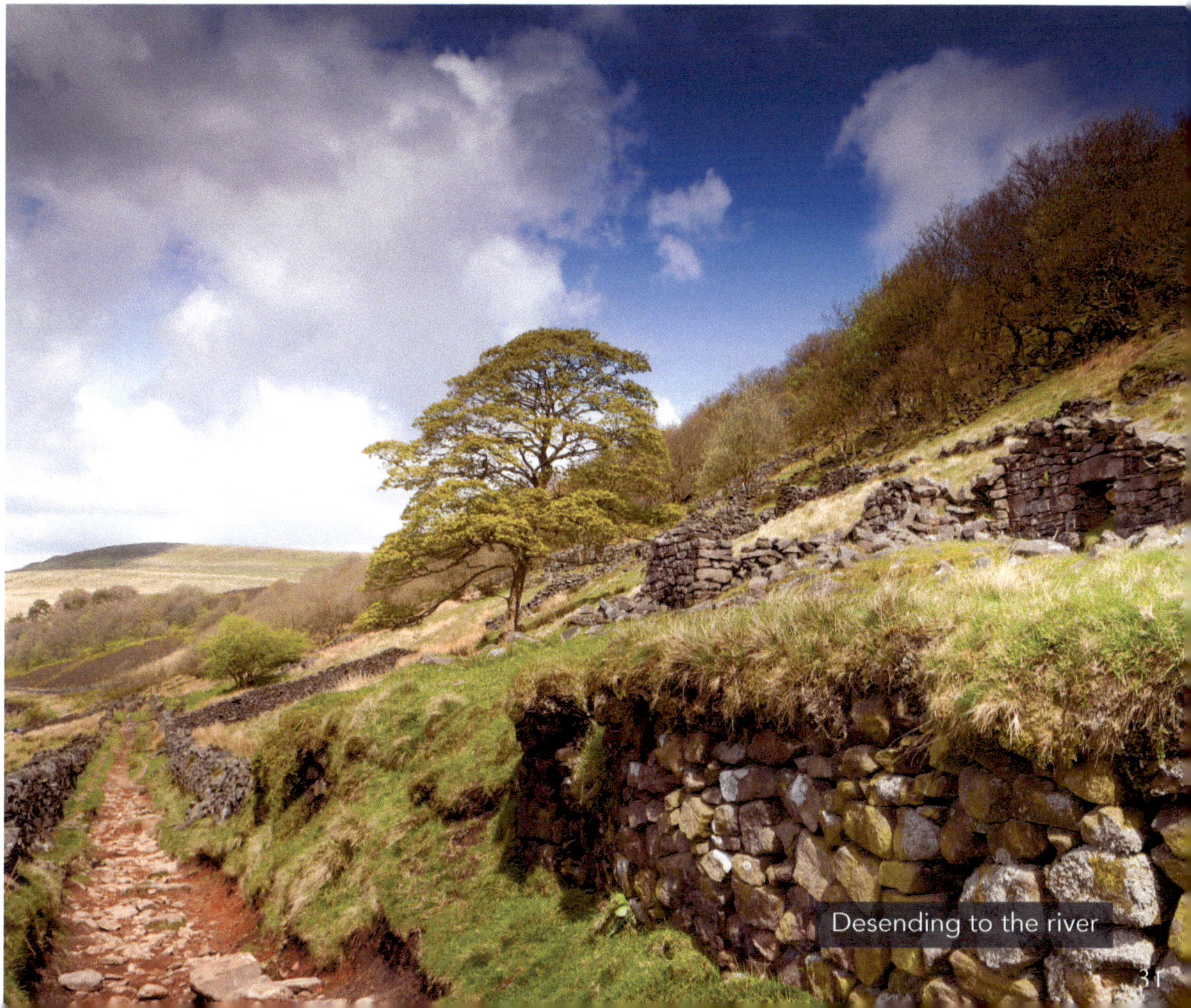

Desending to the river

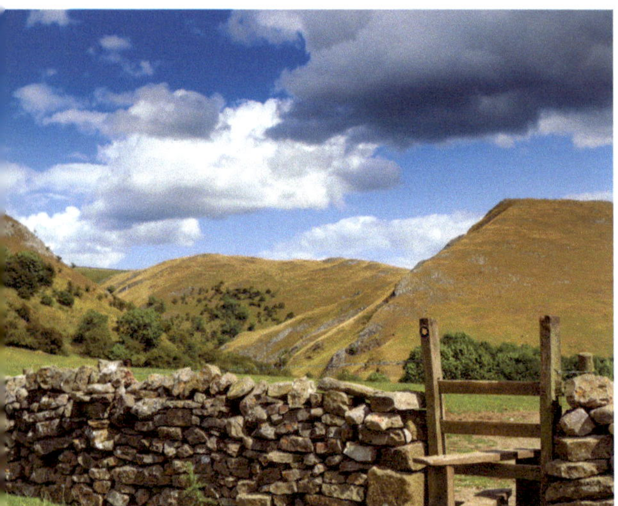

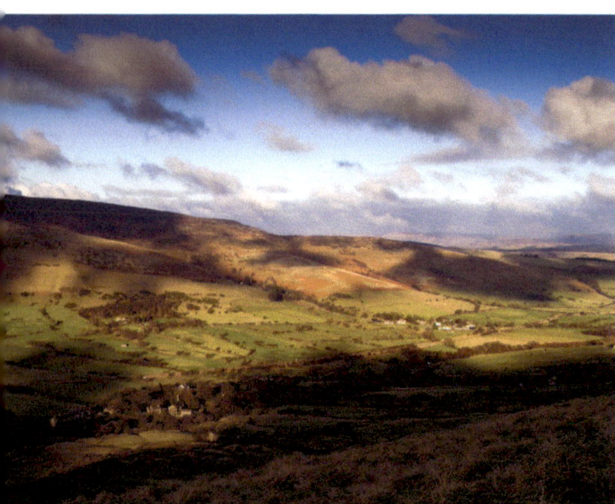

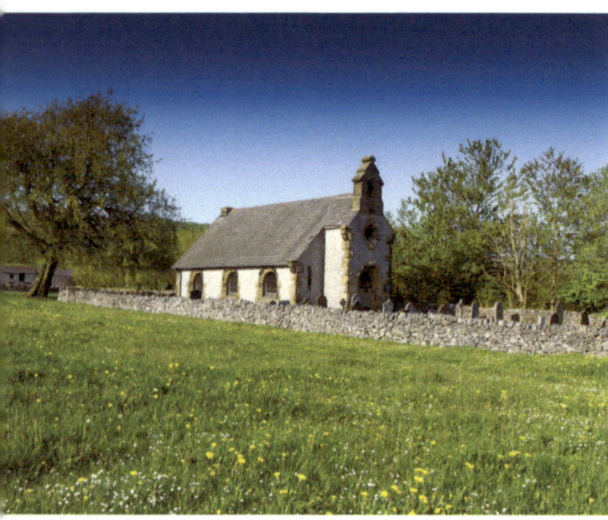

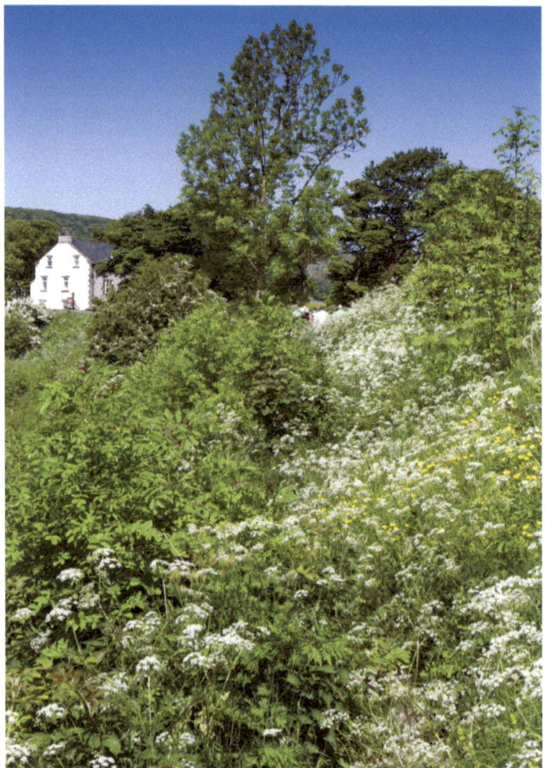

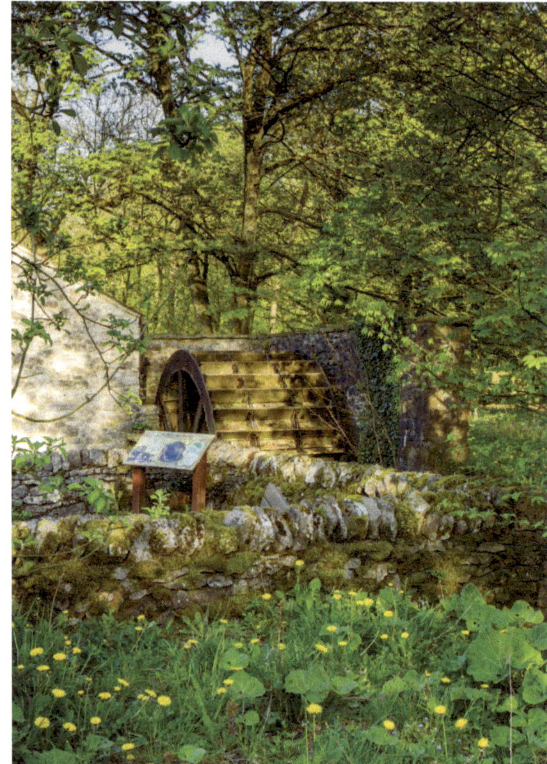

A TASTE OF THE PEAK DISTRICT

DOVEDALE · MONSAL HEAD · EDALE · MILLERS DALE · LITTLE LONGSTONE